ENCOUNTERS *with* NATURE

WHITE STAR PUBLISHERS

Edited by Gianni Morelli

ENCOUNTERS *with*
NATURE

53 OF THE WORLD'S MUST-SEE DESTINATIONS

CONTENTS

INTRODUCTION

Points of contact, meeting places: where the privilege of living on this fortunate speck of universe called Earth is transformed into a magical, unforgettable experience. The landscapes of our planet are kaleidoscopic, changeable, surprising, symphonic, gentle, majestic. They are so varied in relation to our faculties that often we can travel through them only with special equipment or technology. And there are many places where nature surrounds us, amazes us, and conveys intense emotions that in the daily routine of life we often forget. Even though we do not realize it, nature often bestows upon us a reassuring sense of belonging. In this volume we have tried to move forward: not to limit ourselves to describing a unique landscape, but to bring it closer, to let ourselves be immersed in it.

Thus, for the meeting places we have sought still more special ones. We have called them contact points, points where the physical, mental and emotional distance between us and nature becomes so small that it almost disappears. This is the contact: with all the necessary senses in a given situation, plus imagination, which is not indispensable but highly advisable. Also because many of these points are on the border between the imaginable and the unimaginable. We have searched our memories, atlases, encyclopedias, the web, and above all the experience of a number of great travelers, journalists, photographers, and geographers, to tease out, from hundreds of possibilities, the most extraordinary ones. But note well: on condition that they were accessible to all, regardless of age or physical fitness (assuming physical health). We rejected extreme activities and,

apart from a few inevitable (but partial) exceptions, greater degrees of difficulty.

In the end, we selected just over fifty, and each one is a spectacle you would probably never have imagined. Because nature reveals itself in the most fantastic guises.

For example, bioluminescence: it is not simply a matter of fireflies. It is in the sea where another numerous population of "luminous" microscopic creatures live. On some moonless summer nights in the Maldives, they can be so numerous as to create an effect called "milk sea." When you dive, you are immersed in an aquatic representation of the firmament. Speaking of the firmament, maybe you're fascinated by the sky at night. If it creates emotions for you that are deep, ancestral, and not easily identifiable, making your tremble before the cosmos, then you really should go to see our home, the Milky Way, the long curve of its spiral. And you can do this in Namibia, for example, where the sky is totally transparent.

Let's speak about a completely different universe: did you know that in the enormous glaciers of the polar regions (and nearby) enormous tunnels are formed naturally, grottoes with blue ice walls; that there are watercourses, underground lakes, long climbs and huge "halls" with high, luminous ceilings?
Or could you ever imagine diving in the northern seas, amid a family of orcas, each one of which 33 feet long and weighing 10 tons, apart from the youngest, over 6 feet long and weighing "only" 440 pounds? And it is not dangerous.
In the same way, perhaps you could not imagine swimming among humpback whales – whose

dimensions it is better to discover after the swim – in the middle of the Pacific Ocean.

Still more animals, but this time on land: polar bears in Svalbard, almost near enough for you to shake hands, or rather paws; or their cousins, the brown bears of the Kamchatka. Or the mountain gorillas, whose gaze is so similar to our own, in the middle of the forest where Dian Fossey protected them for as long as she could. And hundreds of penguins, curious, haughty (funny, too, but you mustn't tell them this), not only in the Antarctic, but also on the island of South Georgia, in the middle of the ocean. And a "carpet" of orange butterflies in Mexico, the monarchs, which fly thousands of miles each year to mate: the ones that leave are different from the ones that return, and yet they never lose their way. They even recognize branches they have never seen. And flowers? There is a lake of lotus flowers to sail among in Thailand. Or the cherry blossoms on Mount Yoshino.

If you love colors, there's a color design extending for about 190 square miles in the middle of China created by nature on the Danxia mountains in Linze. And talking about incredible colors, there is also the Antelope Canyon in Arizona, or the rainbow trees of Hawaii, or the Caño Cristales river in Colombia. While if you want to play with fire, you need the endless volcanoes and lava in Hawaii, or pools looking into hell in Dankalia and thousand-year-old geysers in Iceland. These are only examples, but there is much more in this volume.

Today global tourism and ease of access to means of communication lead millions of humans to travel the planet. Thus, although the concept of "remote" has gradually weakened, there are still experiences in contact with nature that are capable of leaving an indelible impression upon those who live them, creating moments and memories that can never be forgotten.

This volume, enhanced by extraordinary photographs, presents a selection of the most thrilling natural destinations in the world. It gives invaluable information and advice on traveling to exceptionally beautiful sites and experiencing unique places firsthand.

The boxes, with Advice for Travelers, cultural notes, and inspiring quotations from famous travelers, contribute to making this volume a useful tool for readers wanting to organize a nature trip, or else wishing to daydream before deciding their destination.

Here we reveal many possible destinations, some famous and others less famous. Some have become symbols, while others are more remote.

They are all more fragile than they seem. They must all be protected very carefully while we are still in time. Because we all live on this planet, and we must all do what we can to safeguard it.

Gianni Morelli

4 Nature envelops you in the Thai rainforest.

8-9 High-altitude salt lake: the Salar de Uyuni, in southwestern Bolivia, one of the largest deserts in the world, containing 10 billion tons of salt, of which only a very small proportion is extracted.

ON THE ROOF OF THE ALPS

BEING SLOWLY IMMERSED IN THE WILDNESS OF THE ALPS,
TRAVELING ON FOOT OR ON SKIS THROUGH THE MONT BLANC MASSIF.
HUMANS ARE ONLY TRANSITORY GUESTS AMONG ICE,
JAGGED ROCKS, AND THE LIMITLESS SKY.

The heart of Europe is a granite cathedral, covered with ice, supported by imposing rock walls, and ribbed by a succession of jagged peaks at 13,000 feet. Its architecture, its altitude, its loneliness have made it a mysterious place for millennia, the "*montagne maudite*" inhabited by demons: its glaciers, depicted as dragons, were exorcised by the Savoy parish priests. Then came the Enlightenment,

scientists, and climbers. But still today, besieged with cableways and highways, Mont Blanc remains one of the last corners of wild nature in Europe. It must be approached with awareness and respect.

The most exhilarating excursion crosses the central part of the massif, along the line of glaciers linking Italy to France. In summer, you can do it completely on foot, as in the times of

De Saussure (the Genevan scientist who in 1786 promoted the conquest of Mont Blanc, at 15,700 feet); but starting from

10 Alpine ski mountaineers climb a ridge above the Glacier du Tacul. In the foreground, the Aiguille du Tacul, behind which rises the chain of the Drus, Aiguille Verte, Droites, and Courtes.

11 View from Colle del Gigante, with the Dente del Gigante on the right. The legend relates that shortly before his death the giant Gargantua, created by the French writer Rabelais, ordered that his tooth be buried on the very summit of Mont Blanc.

12 Roped climbers on the slopes of the Tacul; the seracs form labyrinths of towers with fascinating shapes.

12-13 Ski mountaineers on a steep ridge equipped with a manrope : it leads from the cable car summit station of Aiguille du Midi to the starting point for the Vallée Blanche route.

 Humankind needs wild paradises where one does not feel a foreigner on the Earth.

Gaston Rébuffat

French climber and Alpine guide

the first snowfalls and up to late June, many people choose to do it on skis. Today, the Vallée Blanche is a 15-mile off-piste descent (11 miles on the glacier), suitable even for intermediate skiers.

The Skyway is a technological marvel opened in 2015: Its rotating cabins depart from Entrèves, a small village near Courmayeur, and reach Punta Helbronner, (11,300 feet), above the Colle del Gigante. From here you can enjoy a view of the crest of Peuterey and the Mont Blanc peak. Even the "mechanized" part is appealing: It is so fast and

 ## ADVICE FOR TRAVELERS

WHEN TO GO You can do the excursion on skis from the Gigante al Montenvers nearly all year round (best months from March to June) or on foot (from July to September).

HOW TO GET THERE Courmayeur can be reached from Milan or Turin by the highways A4 and A5. From Chamonix, you return to Italy through the Mont Blanc Tunnel.

WHAT YOU NEED Apart from skis, which are always necessary: avalanche beacons, and ice axe and safety rope. For those who are not true experts, an Alpine guide, who can be booked at the Società delle Guide Alpine di Courmayeur or the Compagnie des Guides de Chamonix.

DIFFICULTIES It is a simple trip, about 9 miles downhill. However, it requires perfect physical fitness, training at altitude and familiarity with Alpine equipment.

WEB SITES www.courmayeurmontblanc.it, www.chamonix.com, www.guidecourmayeur.com, www.chamonix-guides.com

14 The Vallée Blanche crevasse, which you meet after the Col du Gros Rognon, in the first part of the excursion.

15 Descent among the seracs of the Gigante. It is the last difficult section before the Salle à Manger, the plain introducing the second part of the excursion along the Glacier du Tacul and the Mer de Glace. The Vallée Blanche descent is now open almost all the year round. Once it was done only in summer by experienced ski mountaineers, but now even novice skiers can accomplish it with hired guides from Chamonix and Courmayeur.

convenient that you are left to enjoy the view. From the station, you immediately set foot on the glacier: in roped climbing parties, with ice axes and crampons, or skiing slightly uphill, you cross the Col des Flambeaux (11,170 feet) and descend through the white desert of the Gigante glacier. The rarefied air and the landscape are breathtaking. In the east rises the lonely Dente del Gigante, in the west the jagged rock wall of the Tacul, a treasure trove of red granite spires and spurs.

Skirting the ever-moving seracs (often you hear the ice creaking, and the distant crack of the ice towers), you continue along the Tacul glacier until you reach the track descending from the Aiguille du Midi. And then you tackle the seracs of the Requin, as far as the level of the Salle à Manger, at the foot of the forest of the Aiguilles de Chamonix. Reaching the Leschaux glacier, you look back and receive a vision of the northern rock wall of the Grandes Jorasses, one of the most majestic in the Alps. Finally you enter the Mer de Glace leading to Montenvers (6,270 feet), among numerous crevasses, under the colossal walls of the Drus and the incomparable pyramid of the Aiguille Verte. At the end, everyone, skiers and walkers, meets up again, somewhere on the Col des Mottes. From here, a path among fir trees leads to Chamonix, but if there is little snow a cableway and a rack railway (the latter opened in 1909) take you back to the Arve valley and civilization.

FINLAND

IN THE FOREST
OF THE SNOW ELVES

SNOWSHOEING IN FINNISH LAPLAND,
WHERE A NATIONAL PARK, THE RIISITUNTURI,
STAGES A SPECTACLE OF THOUSANDS OF SPRUCES
COPIOUSLY COVERED WITH FROZEN SNOW.
IT CREATES AN ENCHANTED FOREST.

There are surreal shapes, as in science fiction or fairy tales. They are shapes that
can thrill you of frighten you, depending on the strength of the light. A mushroom,
a gnome, a joystick. A swan's neck, a dinosaur's head, a penguin, a sheep.
The fat character in a comic, a little monster from the cinema, a poetic bunch of
flowers. No, it is not shadow play on the wall, but Finnish *tykky*. A secular, fantastical
nativity scene, crystallized in white, with shapes that change over a day or a night,
in which we all can recognize something or someone.

16   Cross-country skiers pass a majestic *tykky* in the Riisitunturi National Park. Several days are necessary
for the snow, wind-driven and then frozen, to create these ice sculptures.

16-17   The twilight gives three dimensions to the landscape of "snow guardians."

In lower Lapland, Finland, a few miles from the Russian frontier, the National Park of Riisitunturi (Posio) is the best place to explore this "shape of water." It is special because, around the candle-shaped Norway spruce (*Picea abies*) that grow in the forest, layers of snow are deposited giving rise to white ghosts, as if someone had thrown rumpled sheets on the trees. The cold wind from the Arctic moves the very fine snow and condenses the high humidity, covering the trees that stand in its way. When the temperature falls to between 5 and -22 °F, the white sheets are frozen in their creased shapes, and the sun and the wind on the following days remodel them. In a short time, the taiga is full of strange beings, like the characters of the tales of the North, the snow elves. North-central Finland is a low, undulating land in which conifers and birches coexist to form immense woods, and there are repeated views of frozen lakes, like in a game of mirrors. Over everything, there is the layer of snow that softens, moderates, and puts that harsh landscape into perspective.

An excursion on snowshoes is one of the most magical experiences imaginable: The soft snow sinks with a subtle noise as you walk, the pure Arctic air is warmed in the nose and mouth before being "swallowed," but which gives you a shot of energy; a landscape of lakes and hills and, the incredible *tykky* that seem to be placed there as guardians, or as pilgrims that follow your lead. No one can remain indifferent to this magical atmosphere. Halfway through the excursion, you sit down in the clearing around a hut, you light a small fire to make the coffee and heat up the reindeer stew. Eating in the open air in

the Arctic winter is an experience that adds a charmful element to the outing. It is soft underfoot, not only because of the snow, but also because underneath there is a thick layer of moss, which helps you travel longer distances without your legs feeling tired. The paths marked are the summer/autumn ones, a network of 25 miles guaranteeing a safe and varied visit, and which allow you to take irresistible detours where the thick snow seems like whipped

cream waiting to be "tasted." It is truly marvelous, besides being a very satisfying photographic experience, enabling you to invent personal perspectives and shots. But there is another important aspect: the burden of all that accumulated snow breaks and brings down trees, which in the long run give rise to "elevated" or "terraced" peat lands, spruce and pine trunks in dense aquatic vegetation. This world can be seen in summer and autumn,

WHEN TO GO In winter, from November to April; the most piercing cold is in January and February, and then it gradually eases and the hours of light increase.

HOW TO GET THERE The nearest airport is Kuusamo; then you can rent a car to reach Posio, 40 miles away. The Riisitunturi starting point, the entrance to the park, is near the village of Tolva, but you can also access the park from Kirintövaara.

WHAT YOU NEED Winter mountain clothing. Don't forget a hat, reinforced gloves, mountain glasses, binoculars, and spare batteries for your camera. Snowshoes and rackets can be rented on the spot.

DIFFICULTIES Excursions are suitable for everyone, as long as they are fit and used to the cold.

WEB SITES
www.visitfinland.com
www.nationalparks.fi
www.posiolapland.com
www.northtrek.net
www.rukaadventures.fi
www.polarlightstours.fi
www.basecampoulanka.fi

when trips are organized to gather the fruits of the undergrowth: blueberries, cranberries, raspberries, and Arctic raspberries.

The National Park, in Finnish Riisitunturin Kansallispuisto and spanning almost 31 square miles, was created in 1982. Riisitunturi can be translated as "hill of hay," suggesting "grassy," according to the Sami language. Actually, it is a barren high point of just 1,500 feet from which, however, a sublime view awaits: an uneven expanse of hills from 1,000 to 1,300 feet elevation, of which a dozen are higher, giving the park its undulating, calm appearance. Then there are the lakes with their round forms, among which Kitkajärvi, a protected and uncontaminated environment with extremely clean and clear water. Obviously in winter it is covered with ice. And at last, them, the snowy guardians. Everything is completely stationary, as if it were in a painting, with as many shades of white as there are in Sami words for "snow."

18 Winds and low temperatures form the landscape of southern Lapland. The red spruces of the taiga are bent under the weight of the snow, until they almost merge into the white background.

19 top Coffee and soup are heated up by using pans and a kettle in the national park: they can prove to be valuable refreshment.

19 bottom The magnificent pink-purple light of the brief dusk on the snow in the park in the early afternoon. It is totally magical.

SWEDEN

TREES SLEEPING

WE'VE ALL DREAMED OF IT SINCE WE WERE
CHILDREN, AND IT IS NOW REALITY IN LAPLAND.
SEVEN CABINS PERFECTLY CAMOUFLAGED
IN THE FOREST: NATURE CALLS, AND CREATIVITY
AND MODERN ARCHITECTURE RESPOND.

If you think of Lapland, what comes to mind is snow, reindeer and the Sami. This is true, but it is not all the story. For example, in a forest in Harads, about 30 miles south of the Arctic Circle, a UFO is placed undisturbed among the branches, a huge nest perches in the trees and a mirrored cube reflects the surrounding landscape, apparently disappearing into it.

20-21 The reflecting surface of the Mirror Cube completely camouflages the structure, which is built around a tree trunk. A wooden bridge leads to the interior, which can house two guests.

21 The UFO room can house up to two adults and three children, who can finally have the (almost) realistic experience of a journey through space.

22 and 23 In the Seventh Room, the structure of 800 square feet placed 33 feet above the ground, access is by a sequence of ramps and walkways. It has wide panoramic windows looking onto the river and in the patio there is a suspended net between the trees. It can host up to five visitors and has a bathroom with a shower. The interiors have been created in wood and materials almost exclusively from Scandinavia.

 ## ADVICE FOR TRAVELERS

WHEN TO GO The hotel is open all year round, but you should know that there are very few hours of light in December and January, while the sun never sets in June and July. The best period to try to see the Aurora Borealis is from mid-September to the end of March.

HOW TO GET THERE There are daily flights from Stockholm to Luleå. From its airport you can reach the hotel by taxi, private car (about an hour's journey) or helicopter.

WHAT YOU NEED Waterproof hiking shoes, layered clothing, warm winter clothing, a torch.

DIFFICULTIES You need to be more or less agile to reach each room; the houses are a few minutes' walk from the reception.

WEB SITES www.treehotel.se, www.swedishlapland.com, www.visitsweden.com

It is the Tree Hotel and those bizarre structures placed within pines and firs (for now there are seven, but the number will increase) are tree houses, created by the genius of Scandinavian architects, each one invisible to the others. This disproves another cliché: modern design does not always coincide with an urban cityscape. Inside the aluminum frame of the Mirror Cube, you breathe the scent of resin issuing from the fir that it is constructed around. The floor of the patio is a net placed between the glass walls of the Seventh Room: you can look down among the treetops, or look up and be overwhelmed by a starry sky.

Certainly, the summer is the period in which the body is most relaxed on the border between earth and sky, but winter, winter is something else. And not so much for the Aurora Borealis, which can be seen only by those who do not expect to. The snow creates an atmosphere that is more of a dream than a fairy tale in the Tree Hotel forest, and also gives you the chance to practice a multitude of activities, like dogsledding, reindeer sledding, fishing in the frozen lakes and the most diverse winter sports. In short, you take a step back and you change into elves, or gnomes, straight out of a fairy tale. The temperatures can fall as low as -22 °F, but the Lapps feel fortunate in comparison to the people of Stockholm, "where the snow comes and goes and it's always so dark." It's true that up here in December the sun sets just after lunch. But when the sun is down completely, you take your snowmobile and venture into the infinite forest, lit up by the full moon in the sky and the snow on the ground: a type of light for which the Sami certainly have a name.

SWIMMING WITH ORCAS IN THE NORTH SEA

THEY ARRIVE SILENTLY FROM THE DEPTHS OF THE ATLANTIC OCEAN. THEY APPROACH THE COAST AND FILL THE NORWEGIAN FJORDS, INTERRUPTING THE CALM OF THE NORDIC TWILIGHT.

Every year, between the end of October and the beginning of February, the killer whales meet up between Narvik, Tromsø, the Lofoten Islands and the Vesterålen Islands, in the north of Norway, following the herring migration. This gives rise to one of the greatest orca concentrations in the world, a spectacle to admire from close up; even swimming among them, in the icy embrace of the North Sea.

These giants eat over 400 pounds of food a day. The feeding preferences vary

24 Near Svolvær, in the Lofoten Islands: tourists watch an orca from a rubber dinghy, the most effective means of approaching the orcas and entering the water.

24-25 Orcas hunting herring, the same diet as the seagulls, which together with the sea eagles follow the migration routes. It is easier to spot these species during the long polar night.

26 Young orcas emerging from the water only 33 feet from the boat. Orcas are very active and curious: besides hunting, they court each other and follow boats' wakes.

27 top A group of divers ready for action. You can use a camera to immortalize the experience, but you should remember that the water is dark, and that the (close) encounters with orcas are fleeting: thus, good results are not easy. It is better to experience the wonder with the orcas themselves.

27 bottom A pod of orcas in the Andfjorden Fjord. These animals have a matriarchal system of hierarchy.

according to area and availability. In the Antarctic they prefer seals, in Canada they sometimes attack other cetaceans, and along the Argentinian coasts they feed on sea lions. Here in Norway it is only herring and they are harmless to man.

The rite begins with a complicated dressing process: insulated survival suit and shoes, dry suit, neoprene gloves, mask and mouthpiece. Once dressed, in the silence of the Arctic dawn – we are well inside the Arctic Circle and the days shorten to only a few hours

of spectacular twilight – you embark to reach the orca viewing areas.

It is difficult to foresee the macro position of the most numerous schools: it changes from one year to the next, and you have to wait for their arrival in late autumn to decide the best places to leave from. In the Lofoten islands and in Tysfjord you will embark from piers where dinghies sway, covered by a layer of ice. Alternatively, there are special cruises in motor-sailers with 5-6 cabins and support boats that can move according to the position of the main

schools. In the last few years, the herrings and the orcas have appeared to gather at the ocean side of Lofoten and the Vesteråle Islands.

It is particularly easy to spot them near Andenes, at the northern extremity of this archipelago, which is less well-known than Lofoten but just as evocative. This town is considered one of the best places in the world for whale watching: if we put the two things together, is it easy to understand why whale watching here is an unforgettable experience. But the motions are the

►► ADVICE FOR TRAVELERS

WHEN TO GO The best period to intercept the orca migrations is from November to February, but the best month is January.

HOW TO GET THERE The nearest reference point is Harstad/Narvik (international) Airport (less than 45 miles from Narvik), in general after a stopover in Oslo.

WHAT YOU NEED Warm winter clothing and thermal boots. You need to take things seriously, as this is the far north in winter. The sea temperatures do not fall to the extremes of the interior, but you may sometimes take breaths of cold air at -4 °F.

DIFFICULTIES The trip is not for everyone. Apart from a specific interest, you must withstand the cold and sailing on the open sea in small boats. And you must be fit.

WEB SITES
www.visitnorway.com
www.orcanorway.info/orca-expeditions
www.tysfjord-turistsenter.no
www.whalesafari.no

same, this seascape is beautiful and mysterious, the adventure remains thrilling. You sail, you watch, you wait.

The regulations forbid you to follow the cetaceans: you need to study their movements and position yourself along what could be their route. If the pod, the orca family unit, reaches the boat, at a signal from the guide you slide into the icy water, trying to make the least noise possible. The cetaceans come within a few feet, the males with powerful bodies and great fins, the females smaller, accompanied by

their calves. Then they dive and swim under the privileged visitors: it is a moment that remains impressed forever in your memory. When you climb back on board you're breathless, because of the cold and the emotion. There is something ancestral in this meeting, but the feeling is difficult to describe.

After a few minutes you move on to another point, with another group of orcas. On some days, it takes time to identify a school – orcas are very fast – but when they want to play, it is their curiosity that draws them toward the

boats. Lobtailing (repeated and noisy beating of the tail fin) is also a way to communicate anger, pain and joy.

To "talk" they emit a sound, a sort of plaintive whistle. If you listen carefully once you're in the water, you can hear it. Snorkeling is not the only way to enjoy this spectacle: you can choose between a photographic safari in a dinghy or one on board a motor vessel of about 100 feet, like the ones available at Andenes, which are ideal for those who do not want to go into the water.

NORWAY

FACE TO FACE WITH THE POLAR BEAR

IT IS THE KING OF LAND PREDATORS:
TO MEET IT IS A THRILL AND A PRIVILEGE,
AN ADVENTURE TO EMBARK ON WITH CAUTION
AND RESPECT. SVALBARD IS CONSIDERED
THE IDEAL DESTINATION IN THE POLAR REGIONS
FOR A CLOSE ENCOUNTER.

Svalbard comes from a far-off place. It seems that they set off from the Equator 350 million years ago. The destination was the North Pole, which, according to the geologists, will be reached in another fifty million years.

To reach Svalbard, you undertake a long journey and move along slowly, to respect the epic greatness of a landscape made of ice, mountains and silence.

28-29 Polar bear taken with a fish-eye lens, which curves the line of the horizon.

29 The Austfonna Glacier, one of the largest in Europe, extends for many miles along the island of Nordaustlandet; like many, it is at risk from global warming.

WHEN TO GO In spring, preferably in April, for the snowmobile excursions. From June to September for the cruises, since there is a greater chance of circumnavigating the archipelago completely, crossing the 80th parallel in late summer.

HOW TO GET THERE If you fly, it is also a long journey: you reach Tromsø, the capital of Arctic Norway, via Copenhagen and Oslo. You spend a day there, and finally there is another flight of two and a half hours, at dead of night, to reach this little, remote archipelago halfway between North Cape and the North Pole.

WHAT YOU NEED For the cruise: warm, waterproof shoes suitable for dinghy excursions, windproof pants, a waterproof jacket, a heavy sweater, gloves and a wool hat. For snowmobile excursions: winter mountain clothing, to be supplemented on the spot with a snowsuit, thermal boots, gloves and helmet.

DIFFICULTIES The cruises are suitable for everyone capable of boarding a dinghy and landing for brief excursions. The snowmobile excursions require good physical fitness, a certain stamina and being quite used to physical effort and cold.

WEB SITES
wwww.visitnorway.com
travel.quarkexpeditions.com/ spitsbergen
www.spitsbergentravel.com

◀◀

30 top and bottom Polar bears come right up to an icebreaker near the island of Spitsbergen.

31 The predators are as curious about humans as are the tourists on the boat hoping for the perfect photo.

32 and 33 A bear on a whale carcass; a cub on its mother's back: it will spend its first two years by her side learning to survive.

If you choose the summer, you land in the bewitching light of a sunset that refuses to draw to a close and of a dawn that has already begun. It is never dark in these parts between April and September.

Longyearbyen, the capital of the archipelago in the midst of the Barents Sea, is a mining settlement bent on hard labor and frontier, where the thousand-odd souls living there express, through the little houses' explosive, improbable colors, the will to live and also a certain interest in tourism.

There are essentially two ways to meet a polar bear. In summer, you board one of the cruise ships that circumnavigate the archipelago. You generally leave Longyearbyen behind you, moving on the calm waters of the Isfjorden, accompanied by a few sailboats and a couple of Russian oceanographic research vessels. All around you, as far as the eye can see, there are mountains and glaciers sculpted by a crystalline light.

Usually, the first stage is the Russian mining settlement of Barentsburg,

with signs in Cyrillic, Orthodox churches, Russian schools, mountains of coal and dilapidated transfer lines, where a few hundred Russians live and work in this time warp. The voyage continues, with alternating stages in protected waters and on the open sea, along the western coasts of the archipelago.

Toward the north, you sail by the island of Prins Karls Forland to see the spectacular Magdalenefjorden. At one end of the Liefdefjorden, the ship drops anchor opposite the Monaco Glacier, which emerges from the sea with a front of 3 miles.

On board a Zodiac you come within sight of ice walls that are even more majestic when seen from the water. It is enough to switch off the engine to realize that the ice is alive: explosions, thuds, sinister creaking and then, unexpectedly, a great ice pillar breaking away. It descends slowly, almost elegantly, toward its mortal embrace with the water. It is the birth of an iceberg: it will melt and slowly disappear as it wanders at the mercy of the currents.

It is precisely during the dinghy excursions that you are most likely to meet a polar bear. It is usually mothers and cubs, or individual bears that hunt along the coast. What is more extraordinary and rare is to spot bears that have killed their prey or are about to do so. In these cases, the dinghies switch off their engine and you silently watch the rite of life and death.

What is more extraordinary and rare is to spot bears that have killed their prey

or are about to do so. In these cases, the dinghies switch off their engine and you silently watch the rite of life and death.

You sight belugas, whales, orcas and even, rarely, a few narwhals. The report published in 2015 by the Norwegian Polar Institute describes a surprising situation: compared to the previous census of 2004, the polar bear population in this remote archipelago has increased by 42% and manifests an excellent state of health and nutrition. These data show the opposite trend to the general situation of the Arctic lands, where the polar bear is in crisis owing mainly to retreating ice caused by global warming.

The other way to see polar bears requires a certain sense of adventure. You need to arrive in Svalbard in spring, ideally in April, when the days lengthen so rapidly that in a single vacation you see the night disappear. The temperatures are no longer prohibitive, although they stay well below zero. In this case, you make your base in Longyearbyen and go on excursions for one or two days, just to follow the bears.

The technical and thermal equipment is supplied on the spot together with a snowmobile, which you can choose whether to drive or leave to a professional. The guides are particularly professional, always armed, and used to the harshness of this nature here. The bears must be approached very cautiously, following the guides' orders closely. It is a thrilling and unforgettable adventure, with a very high chance of success, but it must be undertaken responsibly. You must remember that in addition to being dangerous to people, a bear forced to defend itself is generally shot; even stress due to flight may cost the mother precious energy and make her less efficient in hunting. Also in these latitudes, and in these climates, it is crucial that humans be humble spectators and never intrusive protagonists.

Apart from the bears, in spring you can visit the spectacular ice caves. They are just outside the city, but in summer are impracticable.

NO MAN'S LAND AND EVERY MAN'S LAND

Situated between 74° and 81° north, Svalbard is more than 600 miles from the North Pole. Its land area is broadly similar to Ireland's and is 60% permanently covered by ice. It officially appeared on maps in 1596, thanks to Willem Barents, a Dutch navigator who came here in search of the North-East Passage toward the Indies, although a Viking document from 1100 contains the note "Svalbard fundi" with reference to a "frozen coast" seen far to the north of present-day Norway.

In 1920 Svalbard Treaty signed by 14 countries, which later rose to 46, gave Norway sovereignty over the Spitsbergen Islands, as they were then called, but guaranteed to all the signatories the right to exploit the natural resources of the archipelago. Due to this curious legal situation, there are neither visas nor stay permits in Svalbard, and any citizen of the 46 countries can freely go to live in these islands provided he or she can find work. Also by virtue of the Treaty, Svalbard is neutral and demilitarized. They are administered by an appointed governor residing in Longyearbyen, there are no municipalities or counties and representatives are not elected to the Norwegian parliament.

ICELAND

FROM THE INCANDESCENT WORLD

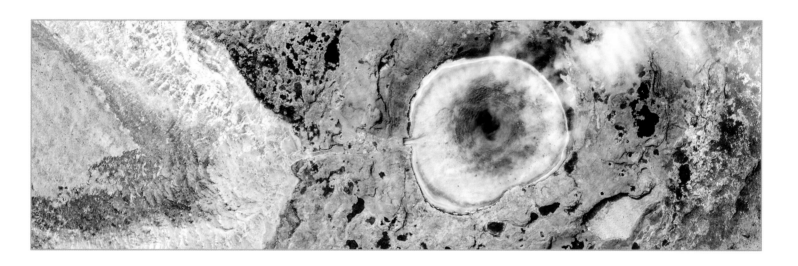

THE WONDROUS BEAUTY OF A GEYSER JET,
A SCALDING BREATH FROM THE FURTHEST DEPTHS,
A CALL TO CONSIDER THE EARTH AS A LIVING ORGANISM.
THIS MAKES US CURIOUS, ENCHANTS AND FRIGHTENS US.

Two drum beats followed by a repressed shout, like that of compressed underground water splitting the air with a dull vibration. Perhaps there is no link between them, but the cry chosen to support the Iceland soccer team in the World Cups recalls that "devil's jet" which is not the only trademark of the island, but expresses its essence: volcanoes and glaciers.

It is precisely the volcanoes, with their enormous power, which can block European air traffic for weeks on end, which are responsible for the geyser, that minor effect, almost a slap from the center of the Earth.

The term "geyser" is derived precisely from the name of the best known,

34 Strokkur, currently the most active geyser in Iceland, with a regular eruption often exceeding 130 feet in height. Every two or three days great explosions occur, caused by the accumulation of pressure.

35 Aerial view of Geysir, the most ancient geyser, in an area believed by geologists to have been active for 10,000 years. It can be recognized at a distance by the bursts of pure steam from the vents.

Geysir, which in turn comes from the verb *gjósa*, "erupt" in Icelandic.

We can explain a geyser in this way: a water cavity is enclosed in a natural syphon, in impermeable rock, which communicates with the outside; the liquid on the outside cools down and that below is heated up by geothermic energy. When the pressure reaches the critical point, it forces the water and steam to issue from the opening in the terrain and thrust into the sky, until the pressure is insufficient to support the jet. It's simple.

The Haukadalur Valley, on the plateau northeast of Reykjavík, offers not only many hot mud pots, but also a clear pool and fumaroles; it also has 1.3 square miles of geothermal field, with the hot springs aligned along a strip 330 feet wide, following the lines of the tectonic plates toward the south and southwest.

Arriving at the Strokkur geyser (in English "butter churn," here a truncated conic vessel) is like preparing yourself to watching a modern circus show, with surprises and incredible performances. There are no barriers or restrictions: you park and enter the area, which seems like any other corner of the island.

Then you see the pool, with people walking around it, waiting for something to happen. They more or less know what it will be like, but not precisely when and how it will take place.

Small bubbles and waves begin to appear, revealing the restlessness underground. They then increase in intensity and size, until the water no longer tolerates those earthly bounds and shoots a clear jet above the crater, to a maximum height of over 100 feet. The water jet is at 257 °F, accompanied by steam, bubbles and wind; it lasts several minutes with

WHEN TO GO Throughout the year, with daylight lasting twenty hours in summer (mid-May- to mid-August) and five in winter. It is a very popular tourist destination, which means that the early morning and the late afternoon are the least crowded moments.

HOW TO GET THERE From Reykjavík airport, renting a car and driving for approximately 62 miles along Route 35 or 36 to reach the geothermic area. Also, round-trip coach tours leaving from the capital stop at Stokkur and Geysir.

WHAT YOU NEED Outdoor clothing, thermal underwear and hiking shoes, windproof jacket, cap, gloves, sunglasses. Weather conditions change often, since they are influenced by the volcanoes. Thus it is always advisable to check the forecast and be ready for any situation.

DIFFICULTIES For everyone.

WEB SITES
www.visiticeland.com
www.visitreykjavik.is
www.icelandtravel.is
www.helo.is
www.re.is/day-tours the-golden-circle

2-3 peaks and then suddenly stops, as when a fountain is turned off. *Voilà*, that's the show. It begins again after 5-7 minutes.

The geyser began to be active in the year of the French Revolution, and this too is suggestive.

Around Strokkur there is the Great Geysir, the original one, which was formed in the thirteenth century as the result of an earthquake and documented in 1294. It was the geyser *par excellence* and reached as high as 260 feet; a spectacle that must have been amazing in the past, but which has now used up its driving force, so to speak, like an unfashionable idea.

Now the jet is much reduced and rare. And then there is the Litli Geysir, and many other *bonzai* mini-jets a few dozen inches high, which are all part of the same "family"!

The area can also be explored by helicopter tour, which offers a view of the entire geothermal area. The island, on the edge of two plates, enjoys the benefits of heating from layers deep under the ground, so much so that even bananas are grown in hothouses. At the same latitude as Greenland!

36 The column of water erupting from Strokkur in the middle of the Arctic night. The phenomenon, also described as the Midnight Sun, enables us to enjoy the endless sunset with the sun motionless on the horizon.

37 top A thermal pool at Geysir: its movements are the sign that a burst is imminent.

37 bottom A water bubble at the exact moment when it explodes, due to pressure from the underground siphon.

ICELAND

IN THE HEART OF THE GLACIERS

WALK THROUGH SPECTACULAR IRIDESCENCE AND INFINITE SHADES OF BLUE IN THE GROTTOES THAT DESCEND INTO THE HEART OF THE COLD.

Ice grottoes: even by themselves, these two words arouse our emotions, make us curious, afraid, excited, and make us imagine. Just think: in Iceland, the real grottoes exceed all our expectations. Because you walk along long natural tunnels that have formed in the immense deposits of ice, in silence, in the freezing cold, through time. You enter cautiously, and you shiver when the daylight disappears behind you. It isn't only the cold. The ice forms curved lines that are also unnatural; crystallized walls, vaults and cascades. They could be the drawings of a megalomaniac graphic artist.

38-39 The color inside the Svínafellsjökull Glacier is due to complete absorption of the chromatic spectrum by the ice: apart from the blue, which is the most penetrating radiation.

39 Guided visit to an ice tunnel. Ice grottoes are a natural, constantly evolving phenomenon: for this reason, it is necessary to observe strict safety rules.

ADVICE FOR TRAVELERS

WHEN TO GO The artificial tunnel in the Langjökull can be visited all through the year; booking is necessary. For the natural glacial grottoes, the best period is from December to February.

HOW TO GET THERE Many organized excursions leave from Reykjavík, the capital; for the Langjökull glacier, they also leave from the nearby locality of Húsafell or the base camp of Klaki near the grottoes. Some of them are open temporarily, and the visit is selected by experienced local guides on the basis of current safety conditions.

WHAT YOU NEED It is advisable to take warm clothes to protect you from humidity, wind and rain; waterproof hiking shoes, gloves, and hat; a camera with good night sensor. The equipment necessary, mainly helmet, torch, and crampons will be supplied by the organizers.

DIFFICULTIES Suitable for all, youngsters included.

WEB SITES
intotheglacier.is
adventures.is/iceland
www.extremeiceland.is

The chromatic contrasts are violent: the dazzling white and very deep blue, the most total darkness and the fireworks created by reflections and refractions of light.

Inside the glacier there is deep silence, but if you listen carefully you can even hear the voice: creaking, drops of melting ice . . . perhaps because the rapid pace of climate change is also reaching the heart of the white giant.

They seem to be ancient, eternal, immobile giants, but glaciers are really currents moving slowly and incessantly downwards. They were formed through the compacting of the lasting snow: after every summer, the remaining snow is buried by subsequent snowfalls and made progressively denser by its own weight. When the ice is subjected to heavy pressure, it melts: it is pushed downward, season after season,

and partly melts. It then finally re-crystallizes in the purity of its magnificent, characteristic blue.

Therefore, glaciers are stratified formations, composed of snow of various ages, up to hundreds, or thousands of years, and even more for the thicker ones: in short, they are equivalent to long recording tapes on which the climate history of the planet is recorded. An excursion inside them is also a

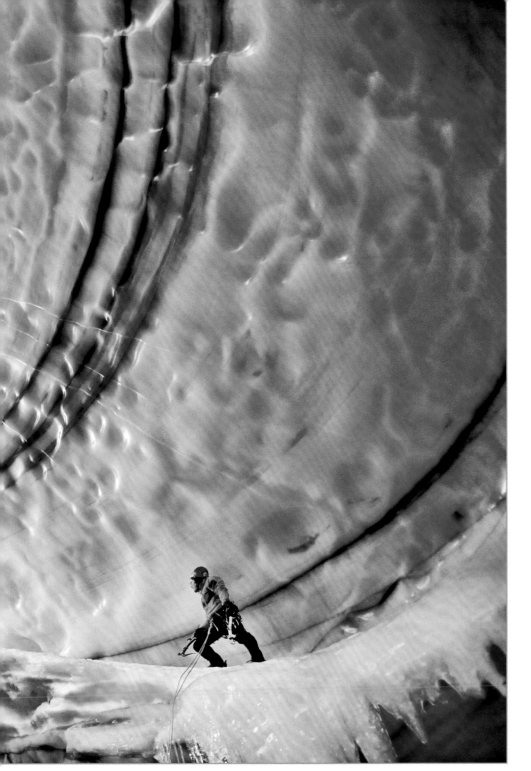

ICELAND: THE EXCEPTION

Iceland, the freezing land, the land of wonders and many records, is an exception for many reasons. First of all, there is the uniqueness of the phenomena and the landscapes created by the coexistence of a long section of the Mid Atlantic Ridge and a geological hotspot.

Without going into much into detail, we can say that incandescent material is emitted from both these "cracks" in the earth's crust. In particular, the hotspot is an enormous underwater furnace: is produces basaltic lava, which rises directly from the bowels of the planet. Iceland emerged from the ocean thanks to all of this: it has been built millennium after millennium by the fire of the planet.

journey through time, a sort of "white archaeological expedition" toward the era of the island's first inhabitants and even before that. It is an adventurous journey for many reasons, first of all safety conditions – dependent on seasonal variability and imperceptible but giant movements of the ice– that only experienced guides are able to assess.

Do not to miss the Crystal Cave,

within the Skaftafell National Park, on the south side of the island, but also the numerous grottoes along the Vatnajökull glacier. But what is unique in the world is the artificial tunnel, 1,600 feet long, opened in 2015, which plunges directly into the bowels of the Langjökull, the second largest glacier on the island.

The journey to reach the glacier is itself is an experience: over 80 miles from Reykjavík, first by bus and then

by tractor adapted for extreme climates, with four-wheel drive and tires that can be deflated while traveling.

40-41 Grotto in the Langjokull glacier: at this point, there are 100 feet of ice above the climber.

42-43 The entrance to the grotto in the Fjalljökull glacier. There are all the shades of blue in the light refractions on the walls.

WHERE ICEBERGS ARE BORN

ALONG THE WEST COAST OF GREENLAND, THE LARGEST
ISLAND ON THE PLANET, AS FAR AS THE ARCTIC.
ALMOST 3,000 SEA MILES FROM THE CEMETERY OF THE
WHALERS TO THE PACK ICE OF THE 80TH PARALLEL, WHICH
CAN BE APPROACHED ONLY ON BRIEF KAYAK EXCURSIONS.

There is perfect silence on this Arctic sea; the perfectly calm water is like glass. A rare occurrence when you think that we are in Melville Bay, between western Greenland and Baffin Island, in the Canadian Arctic. They call it the bay of storms, the whalers' cemetery.

It certainly does not seem so, when seen from a kayak. A handful of these light craft follow the leader in loose formation. Around them is a surreal world of ice sculpted into the most daring shapes: small icebergs and shards from giants; it is advisable to maintain a distance. They are giants with clay feet: 90% of the mass is under water, but erosion and wind make them unstable and dangerous. It is better to give them a wide berth and to paddle in the forest of white pinnacles which, by the way, when seen from the water suddenly appear more imposing. The regular cadence of the paddle, interrupted by the blow of a whale that in the silence

44 The increased density of the pure ice in relation to the water allows these immense mountains of ice to float for 90% of their volume.

45 Kayaking on the silent, pristine Ikasartivaq Fjord.

seems extremely close, leads to a pebble beach and smooth drops of ice.

You land at Dundas (76° 32' N), an abandoned village since 1953, when the Americans built a military base nearby and evacuated the inhabitants. They were faced with a forced transfer on dog sleds 37 miles northward where present-day Qaanaaq is located. The site is of historical importance because the remains of the "Thule Culture" can be found there, an Inuit settlement active from 1100 until 1500,

and because the Danish explorer Knud Rasmussen founded his trading post there in 1910.

You slowly return to the ship and do not realize how many hours you have spent: in this season, the sun never sets, and it is easy to lose your sense of time.

You travel on the *Fram*, a postal boat and cruise ship of the Norwegian operator *Hurtigruten*, one of the few passenger ships that navigates the coast of Greenland. Perhaps the Vikings who arrived here shortly before the year 1000

called it "Grænland," green land. These first discoverers landed in one of the southern valleys where vegetation was always present in summer. They stayed for 500 years, continuing to import, from across the sea, almost everything they needed, from grain to livestock and wood for building. In Greenland, living conditions are not easy and need a level of integration with the environment that the Vikings never achieved: even though it was green, for them this land always remained hostile.

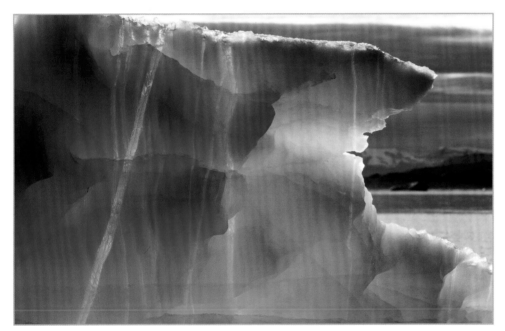

▶▶ ADVICE FOR TRAVELERS

WHEN TO GO The best time is from June to September, to avoid the lowest temperatures.

HOW TO GET THERE On Air Greenland departing from Copenhagen.

WHAT YOU NEED For the cruise: warm, waterproof shoes, suitable for dinghy excursions, windproof pants, a waterproof jacket, a warm sweater, gloves and a wool hat. For kayak excursions: thermal underwear. Survival suits are supplied when the kayak is hired.

DIFFICULTIES These are freezing waters, and it is better not to capsize. Even though the guide guarantees that excursions will only take place in perfect weather conditions, you need a lot of experience in kayaks on the open sea.

WEB SITES
www.greenland.com
www.kangia.gl
global.hurtigruten.com
www.airgreenland.com

Today you come to Greenland for the glaciers plunging into the ocean, for the great icebergs floating everywhere (it is believed that the one that tragically met the Titanic came precisely from here), as evanescent as poems written in water, giants destined to vanish into thin air, leaving no trace.

In particular, in this area, to observe those from Ilulissat: they arrive like silent colossi from the glacier Sermeq Kujalleq, which moves at the speed of 62 feet per day; more than an Alpine glacier in one year. The result is a kind of natural workshop that generates one iceberg after another.

Navigating in such an ever-changing setting is incredibly thrilling. It is the spectacle of the force of nature: as you move, you are accompanied by bursts and roars in a gigantic, enchanted world where the moments of silence are explosive and deafening.

You completely lose your sense of direction, since you are overcome with shapes, lights, shadows and fleeting perspectives. A Unesco World Heritage Site since 2004, the Ilulissat Icefjord is all you need to come this far.

46 Blocks of ice modeled by erosion and thaws, carried on the ocean current.

47 top Kayaking among the icebergs requires good skills, control of the boat, and the presence of an experienced guide who can read and interpret ice conditions.

47 bottom The natural phenomena of blue ice occurs when snow is compacted and becomes part of the iceberg itself. The internal temperature of an iceberg varies between 5 and -4 °F.

ETHIOPIA

BEWITCHING AND INHOSPITABLE DANKALIA

BLAZING LANDSCAPES, ARID STRETCHES OF SALT, PERENNIALLY ACTIVE VOLCANOES AND SULFUROUS GEYSERS FED BY BOILING WATERS; DALLOL AND ERTA ALE, NIGHTMARES OF FIRE THAT SHOW THEMSELVES SHAMELESSLY.

When you visit Dankalia you can confirm that it is a living creature: terrible geological phenomena happen day after day. You feel the earth vibrate under your feet, you watch the waters of the geysers dance, you see on sulfur evaporate and iron oxides being deposited in the foam-covered waters of lakes, and waves of lava from the volcanoes crash into the rocky beaches.

48 Mineral deposits in the Dankalia depression. Owing to the activity of three different tectonic plates, this hollow is many feet below sea level.

48-49 Sulfur springs at the hydrothermal site of Dallol, one of the hottest places on the planet.

ADVICE FOR TRAVELERS

WHEN TO GO   The best period is from November to the end of January; with an average temperature of 94 °F, Dankalia is the hottest place in Africa. The temperatures vary from 77 °F between September and March, the rainy season, to 118 °F, with extreme peaks of up to 176 °F, between April and August, the dry season.

HOW TO GET THERE   The road descending from Addis Ababa (over 6,500 feet) toward the Rift Valley is well-paved: it crosses the desert as far as Lake Afrera. From here, the roads are winding, dusty and rough, with off-road sections on difficult terrain. It is better to contact specialized agencies, accompanied by local guides and an armed escort; you can only camp near police posts.

WHAT YOU NEED   Practical outdoor clothing, light hiking shoes, headlamp, medications for personal use unobtainable *in loco*. Antimalarial medication is recommended.

DIFFICULTIES   A hard, demanding journey, exhausting because of the hours of hiking at extreme temperatures; ability to adapt to an inhospitable environment is necessary. Not suitable for children.

WEB SITES   www.ethiopia.travel, www.dankalia.com

50   The fiery spectacle of Erta Ale, the volcano 1,900 feet above the Salt Plain. It is in the middle of the eponymous mountain chain: on its escarpments sediments of coral emerge, demonstrating how this area was once covered by the Red Sea.

51   Notwithstanding the exhausting conditions (in the hottest periods, the temperatures reach 122 °F), the Ethiopians still work the mineral deposits today.

This is where the African Rift Valley begins its journey, where the three tectonic plates meet. Between Dankalia and Djibouti, Africa is separating from the Arabian Peninsula by 0.8 inches a year, splitting in two at the "incredible" speed of 0.04 inches per year. In practice, in 30 million years a new sea will separate East Africa from the rest of the continent, and Dankalia will return to the bottom of the ocean.

Actually, all of Dankalia is a giant contact point with nature, and the heart of this primordial reserve is the salt desert which extends as far as Eritrea: approximately 463 square miles, of which half constitutes the salt plain. For millennia, dromedaries have transported tons of salt from here to the tableland. There is so much salt because Dankalia is a deep depression, a seabed that dried out about 200,000 years ago, leaving a desert over 330 feet below sea level.

In this curve of the earth, however, there are two particular monsters which await the curious and the bold: Dallol, a volcanic crater called "the land of spirits," the chaotic palette of a distracted painter, and Erta Ale, the volcano that lets you hear the breath of the earth. Around them, there is terrain covered with mineral deposits. Iron oxides, sulfur, magnesium, and sodium carbonate, crystallized, solidified, and liquid, give rise to a landscape in yellow, green and ochre, which blend into one another. An extraterrestrial landscape in which you should move with care and keep your mouth closed despite your amazement.

The Dallol is a Satanic creature, the result of the creative delirium of nature, a concentrate of primordial liquid. Everything boils up, moves, crumbles, evaporates, evolves. It is pure imagination, color, disturbing beauty. For the geologists, it is a collapsed volcano that has emerged on the surface in the form of an infinite number of small geysers fed by the magmatic fault. Here the landscape changes continuously. New formations and concretions grow, combine, become denser, create cones and lakes. Micro-volcanoes are suddenly born from nothing, which belch vapors and waters

THE AFARS AND THE SALT TRADE

On this frontier of fire, more than a thousand years ago after an epic migration, the Afar ("free man"), a Muslim people of Cushitic origins, chose to settle and to adopt the strength, beauty, brusque and intractable ways, eternal silences and sudden generosity of the land. A million and a half people scattered in nomadic clans in a semi-desert region, where only a few small dracaena trees and succulents manage to grow. This is a choice that has led the Afar to model their way of life by linking it inextricably to the mapping of water pools and to seasonal pastures. Their economic and social balance follows the rhythm of the rains. And of salt: work that requires an immense effort, but that has guaranteed an invaluable trade for millennia.

52-53 Overlapping salt sheets on Lake Karoum. Since the rain has softened the surface, the miners can work more easily.

53 top Some workmen extracting salt blocks. In the sixth century, the Egyptian historian Kosmos wrote that the kings of the city of Axum traded salt for gold. While today the value of salt has "depreciated," it continues to be in demand.

53 bottom A caravan of dromedaries transporting blocks of salt toward the market in Makallè: for many Afar tribes, it is an important source of income.

and then vanish. The lakes are among the most incredible spectacles, because the acid colors are combined with the movement of the waters, which are green or yellow, the white sulfur foam and the fumes from everything.

The "smoking mountain," Erta Ale, rises around 2,000 feet from the Salt Plain. This is only accessible on foot; it is the most active volcano on the planet, and among the four in the world with a continuously boiling caldera of lava. The excursion requires three hours' hiking along a path through dark lava with curious shapes, in which you can sometimes distinguish the shape of a hand, a fish, a camel, a cobra's head . . . The only real living forms are the roots of pale green bushes and some acacia trees. Ahead of the tourists, camels walk laden with mats and provisions, because on the summit of the volcano there is no village, only a few uninhabited huts in which to take shelter from the night wind.

Departure, permits and an armed escort are granted by the Afar authorities. It always takes place in the middle of the night (the daytime heat would be unbearable): a night-time hike around lunar, Dantesque landscapes. It is impossible to forget.

Erta Ale is a classic shield volcano: the temperature of 2,192 °F enables the lava of the crater lake to remain in a permanently liquid state.

You make the steep descent into the caldera, and then in a few dozen minutes you cross some lava fields until you reach the lava lake, whose diameter is 260-330 feet. The sight of red lava boiling in the caldera at night is hypnotic and frightening. Millions of years of history and ancestral terror paralyze your thoughts.

MEETING
MOUNTAIN GORILLAS

IN THE IMPENETRABLE EQUATORIAL AFRICAN
FOREST LIVES THE GORILLA BERINGEI BERINGEI,
A GENTLE PRIMATE WHICH SUSTAINS ITS GREAT
MASS WITH A RIGOROUSLY VEGETARIAN DIET.

They are land animals, which above all feed on herbs, flowers, roots and shoots, weigh
from 220 to 330 pounds, and have movements similar to those of humans.
Mountain gorillas have shorter arms and longer fur than other subspecies and live
in groups of around thirty, dominated by a large male that naturalists call a "silverback,"
because he has a silver streak along his back. The leader oversees everything, including
defense, and leads the "family" in an area of between 1 and 2 square miles.

   For human visitors, the most disturbing feature of mountain gorillas is their nearness
to our ancestry shown in gestures, gait, movements, facial expressions, and gaze.

54 Mutual attraction: a young tourist and a gorilla watch each other in the Park of Volcanoes in Rwanda,
with vegetation comprising mainly rainforest and bamboo.

54-55 A family of mountain gorillas relaxing: during the rainy season, it is easier to eat undisturbed from
nature's cupboard.

ADVICE FOR TRAVELERS

WHEN TO GO It is best to avoid the months of April and May, which is the rainy season.

HOW TO GET THERE The nearest airport to the park is Kigali; a 30-day entry visa can be requested at the airport of arrival. The bus transfer from the capital to the district of Ruhengeri (Musanze) near the Volcanoes National Park takes about two hours.

WHAT YOU NEED Sturdy hiking shoes, extendable walking sticks, spare clothes and drinks, light snacks, sun protection creams, hat and binoculars, light raincoat.

DIFFICULTIES Medium: you need to consider two to eight hours of hiking in the rain forest, in a hot, humid climate.

WEB SITES
www.virunga.org
www.rwandatourism.com
www.rwandagorillasafari.net
www.fivevolcanoesrwanda.com
lebambougorillalodge.com

This nearness includes the fact that their pregnancy lasts nine months, and that the young play all the time, playing tricks on one another. This is the fascinating, or frightening, phenomenon: to come up against Darwin and his theories, to see in a primate a distant relative, a mirror, with whom we have an obvious link. Only a few hundred gorillas are left, so few that the population for some time has been included in the IUCN Red List with the note "critical danger of extinction," for species which number under 2500 fertile animals.

When we think of mountain gorillas, we think of Dian Fossey, the American primatologist who moved to Rwanda to study them in 1966, and who stayed there until her violent death in 1985. She shone the spotlight on these primates, making them her life's mission. When she arrived – at the invitation of paleontologist Louis Leakey, and supported financially by the National Geographic Society – for the local people she was "the woman who lives alone in the forest," a strange character who spent her time studying and protecting the animals: her presence was barely tolerated. But as Jane Goodall has said, without Dian Fossey mountain gorillas would no longer exist today. Her research work was a fundamental, scientific and cultural achievement, due both to her studies and the center named Karisoke, which was built in the rain forest between two volcanoes.

56 A silverback, the male leader of the group, shows his teeth. Gorillas are very close to humans' evolutionary level; some scientists say that we share 98% of our DNA with them.

57 top Two male gorillas face up in a fight for domination. A defeated dominant male is destined to live a solitary life.

57 bottom A gorilla leads his family group in the forest of Virunga, at altitude 8,560 feet.

58 A group of tourists trekking along the park's paths, in search of mountain gorillas. Human beings have nothing to fear from them: gorillas only attack if provoked.

59 A gorilla poses, allowing itself to be immortalized by tourists, as a reward for their long hike. Dian Fossey always fought to enable the primates to live in peace in their natural habitat and to limit drastically the disruption caused by mass tourism.

The real attraction is the gorillas, but if you venture a little further, the setting is extraordinary. The Great Rift Valley is the area of division between the Arab and African tectonic plates, a scar that goes from the Jordan Valley to Mozambique; the western branch, the Albertine Rift, produced the Virunga chain of volcanoes, the Rwenzori Mountains (16,762 feet), and the great lakes. These are spaces with an extraordinary variety of environments, from marshes to snow fields, from lava plains to savannas to the slopes of the volcanoes. The fauna is extremely varied, from mountain elephants to hippopotami, to Siberian birds that spend the winter there. Let us not forget that in 1925 in Congo the first African park, the Virunga National Park, was created here, and that the area is a meeting point of nature reserves (the Rwandan Volcano Park in Rwanda and the Ugandan Rwenzori Mountains National Park in Uganda). It is a harsh but delicate environment, above all because of human destruction, hunting, poaching, and deforestation with the resulting elimination of animal habitat, not to mention the numerous wars and the displacement of human population. It is a dramatic picture for an exceptional setting. After the Rwandan Civil War, the park began to operate again; since 1999, rangers have accompanied international visitors to see the animals in their habitat.

You leave at seven in the morning, in groups of eight led by a ranger. You must follow his instructions, with no independent initiatives. You enter the forest along the paths, in a humid heat that envelopes you like the leaves of the trees. You have a long time to wait, and you may well be disappointed: the ten gorilla families move to gather food, and sometimes seem to be an unreachable goal. The tour is not for the easily discouraged, and requires patience, since you have your goal and know that the rangers will do everything to attain it. Whether you arrive after two hours or even five, it is touching to encounter the animals on the slopes of Mounts Bisoke and Karisimbi, in the midst of the intense green of the vegetation. It is the gorillas who are the hosts, the opposite of what humans are used to believing. If they feel like it, they look at you, they smile, or something similar, they make faces, or grimaces, or make gestures of annoyance. But they are there, in their green home, intent on eating some of the 74 pounds of vegetable matter they consume every day. They do not pose for photos and they do not understand selfies, but they are not disturbed by human presence, provided there are few humans and they are not stupidly aggressive. Sometimes they watch you, as if to try to understand who these furless pale beings are with such similar movements to theirs.

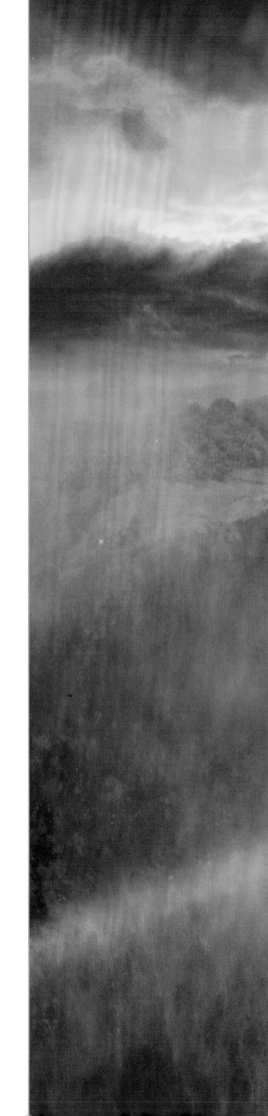

ZAMBIA

VICTORIA FALLS: ON THE EDGE OF THE ABYSS

THE MOST MAJESTIC FALLS IN THE WORLD
SEEN FROM ABOVE, AFTER SWIMMING
TO "THE DEVIL'S POOL" SURROUNDED
BY MIST AND ENDLESS RAINBOWS.

It is a drop of 360 feet, 5,600 feet wide. The largest vertical sheet of water in the world separates Zambia from Zimbabwe and is the break in the 1,500-mile course of the Zambezi from its sources, in the northeast of Zambia, to its mouth on the Indian Ocean. It is precisely this great river that is the protagonist of this adventure. As it was for David Livingstone, on that 16th November in 1855: while paddling his pirogue, following the current, he heard a terrifying noise approaching.

60   The Devil's Pool, the natural pool of the brink of the abyss. In general, this natural swimming pool is open from August to December, when the Zambezi's intensity and level are acceptable.

60-61   The Victoria Falls from the Zambian side. In the mid-nineteenth century, the explorer David Livingston chose the name, in honor of the Queen of Britain.

62-63　The front of the Victoria Falls is more than 1 mile wide.

63 top and bottom　Extreme sporting activities performed in perfect safety have increased the numbers of tourists coming to the falls since the 1980s.

 ADVICE FOR TRAVELERS

WHEN TO GO　The best months are August, September and October.

HOW TO GET THERE　The closest airport is Victoria Falls International Airport, around 12 miles from the falls.

WHAT YOU NEED　Comfortable waterproof shoes (reef shoes are ideal), waterproof bag, swimming suit, sun protection cream, waterproof GoPro or action camera.

DIFFICULTIES　The experience requires excellent swimming ability and no fear of heights, even though the guides are very attentive.

WEB SITES　www.zambiatourism.com, www.victoriafalls-guide.net, victoriafallstourism.org

The falls were then, and still are, one of the greatest spectacles in Africa, signaled by clouds of water vapor visible up to 25 miles away, cloaked in dozens of rainbows and with a maximum flow rate of 320,000 cubic feet of water per second. Recognized as a Unesco World Heritage site, they are set in the Mosi-oa-Tunya National Park (whose name means "smoke that thunders"), with its 25 square miles including the area of the falls and about 12 miles of river on the Zambian side. The park is also home to hippopotami, a great variety of antelopes and also zebras, giraffes, and elephants.

The most classic views of the

cataracts are from Zimbabwe, following the paths though the luxuriant rain forest to the edge of the abyss. If you feel brave, you can go as far as Danger Point, a tiny terrace of slippery boulders on the edge of the canyon. However, you can experience real adventure on the Zambian side if you leave from the pier of the luxurious Royal Livingstone Hotel.

Only during the dry season, and river conditions permitting, you can take a motor launch and cover the stretch of river from the bank to Livingstone's Island. From here, the boldest can swim as far as the Devil's Pool, a natural pool,

sheltered from the strongest currents, on the very edge of the falls. This is an experience only for skilled swimmers, since to return to the island you have to swim in a zigzag line that the guides show you, in order to avoid the currents and possible dangers of the river. It is impossible to describe the thrill of looking over the rim of these majestic falls. The current seems to disappear and the water, unlike at every other point on the rim, tips lazily into the void before suddenly accelerating. Over time, the river has carved a niche under the rocky border with room for your legs, where you feel safe while your arms are resting on the end of the world. All around you, the scene is dominated by rainbows, the roar of the falls, and vapor rising to the sky. Adrenaline gives way to wonder. For this reason, it is better to organize this trip outside the popular periods when you risk feeling hurried by the guides, who have to make space for the next visitors.

The ideal conclusion to this experience is a boat trip along the Zambezi upstream from the vortex. There are Biblical views of the impressive vastness of the river, under limitless skies with continuously moving clouds. The river flows slowly and majestically, marking the tempo of a trip out of time.

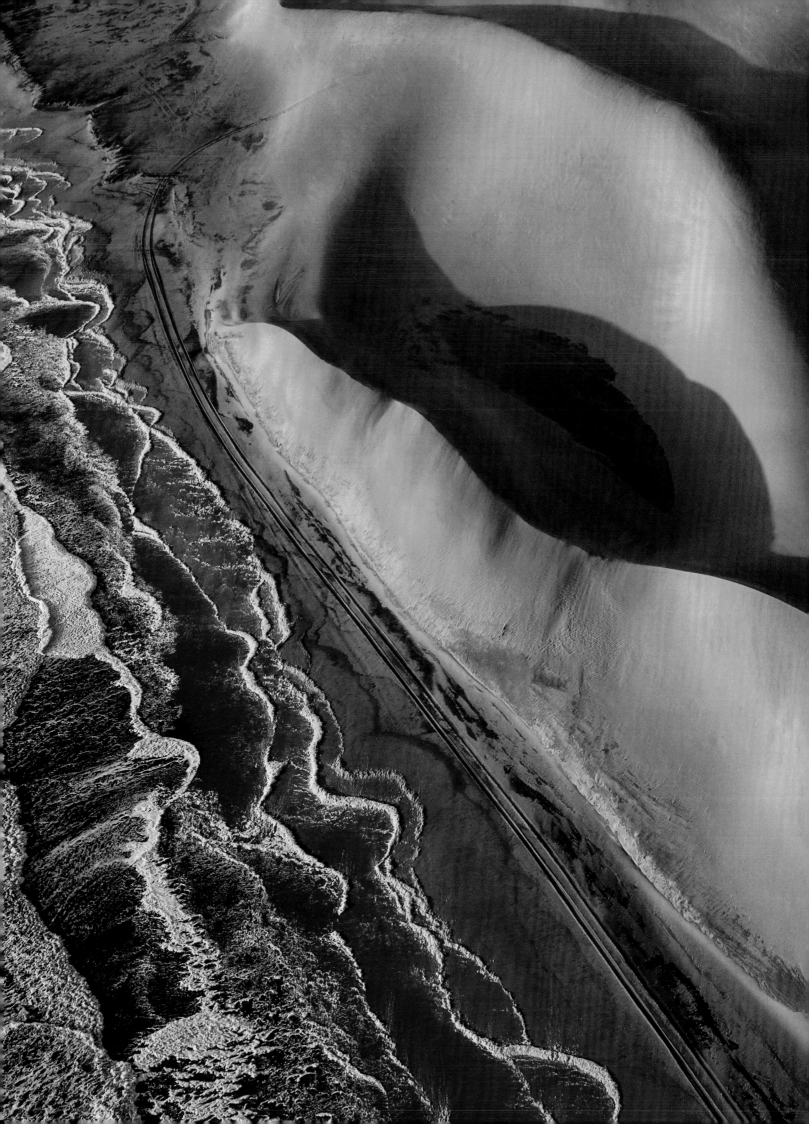

NAMIBIA

THE ROARING DUNES OF THE SKELETON COAST

APART FROM THE COLD ATLANTIC WATERS, THE LONG, DESOLATE BEACHES AND A PAINTED DESERT BEHIND YOU, THE SANDS HAVE ONE MORE SURPRISE: THEY PLAY THEIR INFINITE SONG.

E-F-G is not an advertising slogan for the Namibian coast. It is the series of musical notes in which the dunes of the Skeleton Coast express themselves. The unpleasant name refers to its disarming inhospitality to the shipwrecked: 250 miles of coast without fresh water, with a desert swathe of 6,000 square miles. The name could only be "skeleton," as testified by some rusty wrecked ships a few steps away from the shore.

64-65 A magnificent aerial view of the Skeleton Coast, with the waves of the Atlantic lapping the desert. As you walk on the dunes, you seem to step on a desert lion, which protests as you pass.

65 You can also use a quad to visit the imposing sand mountains in the Erongo Region, near Swakopmund, further south along the ocean shore of the Skeleton Coast.

66 top A desert elephant walks along the bed of the seasonal river Horusib. These elephants have adapted to the desert: they have longer legs and larger feet. They can cover 37 miles a day in search of food, dig holes in dry riverbeds to find water, and go without drinking for four days.

67 A 4x4 on the dunes of the Skeleton Coast. A four wheel drive is the only vehicle that can climb such massive and dangerous dunes.

 ## ADVICE FOR TRAVELERS

WHEN TO GO Throughout the year, avoiding the rainy season, between January and the beginning of April.

HOW TO GET THERE Local airlines from the airport of Windhoek, the capital, lead to the only camp in the area, the Hoanib Skeleton Coast, inside the park. As the area is managed by the government, you need to apply for permission. Guides in 4X4s accompany the travelers during the entire visit.

WHAT YOU NEED Suitable clothing, hiking shoes, extendable walking sticks, binoculars, a hat and sunglasses.

DIFFICULTIES Accessible to everyone.

WEB SITES www.namibiatourism.com.na, www.wilderness-safaris.com

66 bottom A curious meerkat (small desert mongoose) watches a child sliding on the dunes. This species is physiologically adapted to the high desert temperatures and survival with little food.

If, then, the shipwrecked sailors, maddened by sun and thirst, tried to continue into the desert, they found sands that began to sing, evoking spirits or increasing their madness still more. Marco Polo in the Gobi desert had heard thundering sands, manifestations of spirits ." . . like drums or the clash of arms." Of the approximately 30 sites in the world where the sands sing, the Skeleton Coast is one of the most evocative, allowing you to walk, run, and slide down the dunes, dancing to the sound of the sand.

But how can they sing, or roar, on those specific notes?

The Skeleton dunes are quite low and light-colored, and the wind is irregular. This has formed wind designs, curves, ridges, piles, and holes sculpted in the most unpredictable way. When the wind blows the sand to the top of the dune, it accumulates toward the downwind side. The sand does not move: in its equilibrium, it has found its "angle of natural friction." But some sands react unpredictably. At some points – where the sand grains

of the surface are unstable, air is present, or there is low humidity – the fall from the angle of natural friction creates a thunder sound.

It is enough for you to sit and slide, or to walk on it, that compression sets the rubbing of the grains in motion, and the resulting resonance rapidly spreads throughout the dune.

Stationary waves are created that reinforce one another; sometimes the grains are synchronized, and they start to oscillate together, transmitting the movement to the whole dune,

The oasis is made for the body, the desert for the soul.
African proverb

68 Gemsbok, South African oryxes, are common in this part of Namibia and represent the country in its coat of arms. The elegant animal, the largest of the oryxes, has horns 29 inches long; the male can weigh as much as 440 pounds.

69 Tracks left by the desert viper, a small poisonous snake that hides under the sand; its eyes and the tip of its tail are visible, and it feeds on lizards.

which vibrates like a musical instrument. And the notes emitted depend on the size of the grains, while the sound is amplified by the lower part of the dune, in the form of a bowl.

On the Skeleton Coast they say that they roar, like a disturbed or hungry lion, but perhaps it is only the suggestiveness of the place. In fact, the sounds are different: sometimes they recall the milling of grain, the sound of a stream, pearls falling from a necklace. Or the hiss of a snake about to attack or the rustling of cloth. But it can also be loud, impressive, like the beating drum in a band or a summer thunderstorm. As we are in Africa, it can also be interpreted as the spirit of the earth or the god of the dunes, or the souls of the shipwrecked sailors of Skeleton Coast. Everyone applies his or her own interpretation and suggestion. What is certain, or rather probable, is that after some time the grains lose their voice when the silicon layer covering them wears off. Landscape here is transitory, because this is the most inhospitable coast in all of Africa.

THE MOST ANCIENT DESERT IN THE WORLD

To the east, you can reach the desert in a 4X4. "Painted desert" is not a slogan. Black, red, pink, yellow, brown, it seems like a Pantone catalog of nature, not only because of the light, but also the minerals and their forms. Magnetite sprayed like powdered sugar on a valley, as if to define its features, as you do with charcoal when drawing; red and black feldspars as a grit pavement; sands, pebbles, and stones of various dimensions, as in a set of samples. Kopje, that is little hills of granite, eroded, frayed, attacked by lichens, with holes forming arches. Precisely cut basalt, smooth walls that gleam in the sun like ebony. Quartz and quartzite that make the desert gleam like a starry vault or a dazzling celebration. Veins of quartz in the granite, crystallized by pressure. Mica, to create dark tones, and black lines of dolerite, which are the backbone of the desert. The most ancient desert in the world, eighty million years old and still willing to please today.

NAMIBIA

THE MILKY WAY ABOVE THE VOID

THE GREAT CURVE OF THE GALAXY PIERCES THE CLEAR NIGHT
OF THE NAMIB DESERT, ABOVE A BARE LANDSCAPE STRETCHING
TO HORIZONS TOO DISTANT TO BE CREDIBLE.

The immense, uninhabited spaces of Namibia are not subject to mist or light pollution, the two elements that lessen visibility of heavenly bodies. Apart from nighttime fogs along the Atlantic coast, the air is extremely limpid: the aridity of the climate minimizes the concentration of humidity in the air. Particularly on the mountains of the interior, between 4,900 and 6,500 feet, the altitude makes the atmosphere even more rarefied and crystalline. Thus, on the Damaraland mountain chains, facilities have been created – hotels and camp sites – equipped with amateur and scientific telescopes: here aspiring astronomers, or simply curious tourists, can spend their nights exploring the southern sky, while the Namib desert sleeps, waiting for another day.

There are many sensations, and they change during the night. You are alone in front of the firmament, excited by the idea of surprises that the universe could hold it for you: Little green men to communicate with, or gravitational effects that can pierce the time barrier; around you darkness, a few noises from the uninhabited mountain, few movements. You feel fear, happiness, curiosity.

There are endless stars. Among the infinite gleaming stars, the Southern Cross stands out: it is the protagonist of so many sea stories, the celestial compass

70 and 71 Namib-Naukluft National Park: the Milky Way shines above the baobab and aloe dichotoma, a variety of aloe typical of the deserts of southern Africa, which can reach 23 feet in height. It is called the "quiver tree": in fact, the bushmen make quivers from its branches and leaves.

WHEN TO GO The most comfortable period of the year is the southern winter, from June to September. It is dry and relatively cool. However, the daily temperature range is great: at night, the temperature may fall to below zero.

HOW TO GET THERE The International airport of reference is Windhoek, around 124 miles from the desert. Once you reach the entrance of the Namib-Naukluft National Park, you can move around in shuttles or a rented car. There are few paved roads; however the tracks are mostly in excellent condition, owing to very low precipitation. They can be used all through the year. The distances are considerable, but there is little traffic.

WHAT YOU NEED Summer clothing, including a windproof jacket for the nights. Good desert shoes and everything that may be necessary for excursions on foot or by jeep on hot and dry days.

DIFFICULTIES Accessible to everyone.

WEB SITES
www.etendeka-namibia.com
www.tivoli-astrofarm.de/htm_e/e_guestfarm/e_anfahrt.htm
www.hakos-astrofarm.com

of ships on the ocean waves and caravans among the dunes is of the desert.

Then there is Orion, with its tri-starred belt; and Betelgeuse, Rigel, and Bellatrix as accompanying maidens of reflections and legends. And then Sirius, which is found by following the line indicated by the belt. Sirius: white, splendid, the most luminous star in all the earth's sky.

72 top and bottom Solitude, some natural silhouettes on the horizon and the world lit only by the stars.

73 This image of the Milky Way is obtained with a very long exposure focused on Gacrux and Acrux, stars in the Southern Cross constellation: it is the Namibian night.

THE MILKY WAY IN NUMBERS

One point one four billion stars; a number beginning with one and ending in seven zeros. That is the number of stars belonging to our galaxy catalogued a few years ago by the Gaia Mission of the European Space Agency. We familiarly call "Milky Way" the galaxy that is home to us and all the solar system. The strangest thing, if you like, is that scientists estimate that this corresponds to only 1% of the stars in our galaxy. There are so many that to go from one extreme to the other, light would take 100,000 years (light years, obviously).

Perhaps it is better to forget the numbers and limit ourselves to observing this luminous trail across the vault of heaven around us. It is composed of stars to which we have given mythological, historical, fantastical, astrological, and mathematical names: Like V766 Centauri, Antares, La Superba, and Polaris. The largest star is called UY Scuti, while the Magellanic Clouds are small minor galaxies orbiting our own. The largest of the nearest galaxies is Andromeda, a spiral galaxy like the Milky Way. It is two thousand, five hundred million light years from the Earth. The amazement never ends.

BOTSWANA

ON THE GREAT RIVER EMBRACED BY THE DESERT

THE OKAVANGO IS AN ENORMOUS GEOGRAPHICAL ANOMALY: THE RIVER CROSSES SOUTHWESTERN AFRICA FROM ANGOLA TO BOTSWANA, CREATING AN AUTHENTIC DELTA, FULL OF CANALS, ISLANDS OF SAVANNAH, AND POOLS OF CLEAR WATER THAT GENTLY DISPERSE IN THE BRUSHWOOD OF THE KALAHARI.

The *mokoro* is a canoe that glides lightly on the waters of the river, between the high grass and the dense papyri. The green wall of aquatic plants opens up in front of its bow like two great hands with their fingers spread open. Where the stalks are less dense, the water lilies appear on the surface from complex spirals of roots that are clearly visible in the limpid water. Every time

74-75   Canoeing on one of the lagoons of the great river. When the river is in flood, in June and July, the delta expands to as much as 6,170 square miles. Its water is almost immobile, due to the insignificant gradient.

75   The delta is densely inhabited by the fauna of the savanna: here a zebra crosses marshland.

 ## ADVICE FOR TRAVELERS

WHEN TO GO The Okavango is right in the Southern Hemisphere, so the seasons are inverted. Adjusting for the change in climate, the thaw on the mountains of Angola should correspond to autumn. Because of a complex series of geographical-climatic interactions, the flood in the delta takes place between June and August. This is the best season for a visit. The climate is dry, with a very strong temperature difference between day and night (when the temperature can even approach zero); while from the end of November to May it is the period of low waters and excursions are not possible in many camps.

HOW TO GET THERE Flights are from Namibia or South Africa for Gaborone, after which there is a small tourist aircraft to the location chosen as the base. You move in a jeep or by Cessna from one camp to another.

WHAT YOU NEED Suitable clothing, hiking shoes, sunglasses, hat, binoculars for watching animals, and a set of warm clothes for the evening and the night.

DIFFICULTIES Accessible to everyone, but do-it-yourself trips are not advised and still less encouraged.

WEB SITES www.okavangodelta.com, www.botswanatourism.co.bw

the canoe leaps ahead, from somewhere near it there is a frightened flight. There is a little bird smaller than the fist of the guide propelling the *mokoro* with a pole: it is so light as to perch on a papyrus stem. The head, back and wings are the color of Oriental blue silk, which is both deep and bright. In flight, it moves its wings so rapidly that they form a turquoise blur against the sky. No one knows why they called this bird with this brushstroke of color the kingfisher.

All around, you feel the enormous presence of the arid, featureless

Kalahari bush, so traveling by canoe seems surreal.

A gap opens in the reed-beds: a few feet away, a minute island appears with two palm trees, with a pensive elephant beginning to shake one of them: in a few seconds, the roots give way. He buries his head among the branches and re-emerges with an enormous leaf clutched in his trunk, like a mammoth primitive fan.

This is daily life in the delta: you can see the waterbuck submerged up to its nostrils in an attempt to hide, or baboons

crossing the clearing in front of a herd of kudù or impala, or the dark patch of a gnu standing out against an area of grass as bright as noon. They speak of it around the fire at sunset, in the few villages of the Bushmen (the San people inhabiting the Kalahari).

76-77 A "fleet" of tourist canoes on the clear water of a delta arm: you can also glimpse vegetation under the surface.

77 top Where there are great herbivores, there are also great predators: a pride of lions watched from a jeep.

77 bottom A light aircraft flies over the Okavango savanna at low altitude: often tourists are taken from one location to another by these small planes.

They speak in the tourist camps, while around them the sun, below the horizon lights up the sky with that African red that has no plausible imitations, while the fish eagles emit their modulated cry before diving onto their prey, and the minute bell-frogs begin their evening concert.

Later, the silence of the night is occasionally broken by the thuds of breaking trees: the elephants are continuing their work in the dark.

Despite the view from the *mokoro*, the delta, like the elephants, ceaselessly moves in time and in space, in the silent stillness of the reed-beds. And it changes continuously: when the floodwaters from the mountains of Angola arrive, the river swells. New watercourses, new wells, are formed. A lagoon is created where once there was an arid plain, an island grows where the earth has clung to the grass or plant roots. And the delta moves still further south. All of this is repeated every year, and each time the delta assumes different forms. The river transports material that is deposited everywhere, termites construct compact castles of debris, elephants and fire destroy the trees holding a small island together, papyri and reeds build impenetrable natural dams. Thus when the current changes direction, the water goes in different directions and creates new liquid avenues for the *mokoros* and the animals. Even the main canals form a new meander, carve out a new course, suddenly bend to the side when faced with a fallen trunk or vegetation that has rapidly covered it.

And then one flood is never the same as another: there are years when a large volume of water arrives and vast areas of Kalahari are swallowed up by the Okavango, and years when drought weakens the river and the sand sucks it

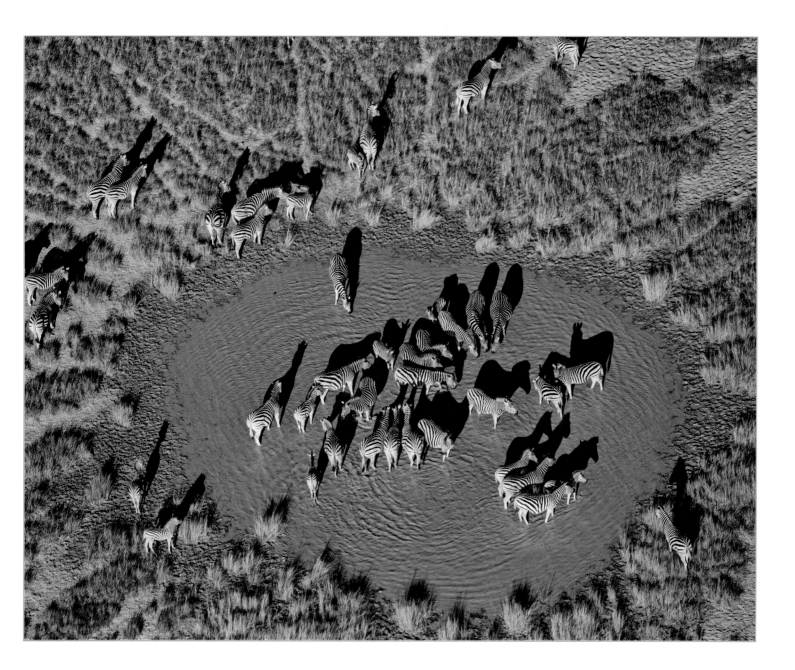

back into the bowels of the earth earlier than usual. In that case, the animals emigrate northward, and in order to survive the hyenas dive to catch fish, defying the hippopotami.

As in the desert, water is the arbiter of life and death. It is no accident that the propitiatory rites for rain of the Mbukushu, who live in the delta, are much respected in all of southern Africa, and perhaps it is no accident that the currency of Botswana is called "pula," the same as "rain" in the Tswana language.

And then in every dry season fire (from spontaneous combustion or started by poachers) burns half the vegetation of the delta for dozens of miles. It meets no obstacles, and in its wake it leaves hundreds of skeletons of trees and carcasses of animals that could not escape.

But this is not all: the earth moves here, too. The Rift Valley shakes the delta with its earthquakes and imperceptible gradients that only geologists understand. Thus, for example, it can happen that some branches of the delta dry up and others, now forgotten, are filled with flowing water again, as happened with the Boro, which had been dry for more than thirty years after the long period of earthquakes in 1952. The bushmen know all this: they have lived here for thousands of years, as have the Mbukushu and the aYei, who both arrived from the north, from the Namibian Caprivi Strip, at the end of the eighteenth century, following a mythical hippopotamus hunter named Hankuzi.

78 A herd of elephants crosses the river delta, known also as the Okavango swamps. They are the true rulers of this land.

79 Herds of zebras drinking, as seen from the plane. Many herbivore species live in this area thanks to the river.

80-81 A hippopotamus in the Chobe National Park, traversed by the River Okavango.

THE FIRST EXPLORERS OF THE DELTA

If you thought that the first white man to see the Okavango was the inevitable, legendary Dr. David Livingstone, then you guessed right: he was coming from the Zambesi and was headed for the Kalahari in 1849. Four years later, the Swedish hunter C. J. Andersson was also awestruck by the magic of the delta. On returning, he related: "Wherever one looked, a sea of fresh water stretched, in many places hidden by clumps of rushes and reed-beds of every color and shade; numerous islands rich in luxuriant vegetation were scattered over the surface and conferred on the whole an indescribable beauty."

However, only later, with the progress of geographical exploration, was the origin discovered of that "sea of fresh water and islands rich in luxuriant vegetation" which coexisted with one of the most desolate deserts on Earth.

By a quirk of nature, which in Africa, more than elsewhere, enjoys playing tricks, the source of the Okavango (or Cubango) lies on the Bié plateau. The river ignores the Atlantic coast of Angola, less than 180 miles away, and begins to descend slowly toward the center of the continent, touches Namibia, and then reaches Botswana where, in an imperceptible hollow only a few feet lower than the surrounding land, it fans out into different water courses, lagoons and islands. In accordance with its duty, as with all rivers in the plain, the Okavango opens its delta, as if it were offering itself to the sea. Yet it disappears slowly in the Kalahari sun, sinking into an ocean of sand and evaporating into the tropic sky.

MADAGASCAR

AT THE FOOT OF THE KARST CATHEDRAL

ROCKY NEEDLES, SUSPENSION BRIDGES
AND DAMP GROTTOES HERE AND THERE
IN A PRIMORDIAL LABYRINTH. A LIMESTONE
MASSIF ERODED OVER TIME, WHERE YOU CAN
MEET LIVELY, BUT SLY-LOOKING, LEMURS.

The starting point is the Morondava trail. It can be muddy or dusty, depending on the period of the year. When the sun is hottest, Morondava becomes a town besieged by dust, sand and time. It is the Far West of Madagascar, the outpost of ancient kingdoms overlooking the Mozambique Channel, facing Africa. Here the Sakalava people settled.

82-83   Despite the long journey required to reach it and its difficult access, Tsingy de Bemaraha National Park receives about 10,000 tourists every year.

83   The River Manambolo flows through the nature reserve; its intense orange color is caused by the slow erosion of mineral sediments deposited on the riverbed.

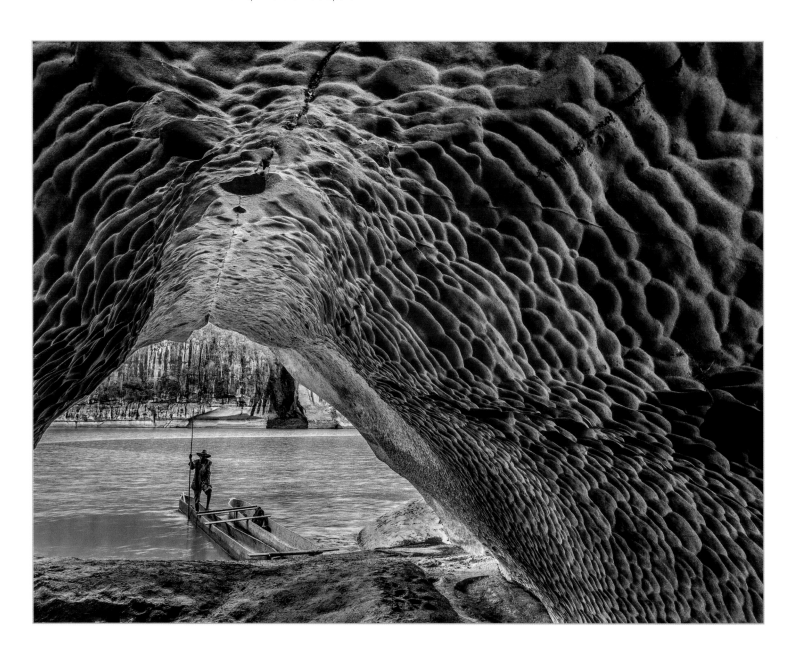

The name means "inhabitants of the long valleys." They have never mixed ethnicity, with isolated pirates or shipwrecked sailors, and their presence seems to give everything a more African flavor. The attractions of Morondava are the Avenue of Baobabs, a red sand trail, and the great mosque recalling local settlements of Yemenite and Comorian traders.

From the city you can reach the Bemaraha needles, which in Malagasy are called *tsingy*. They seem like the spires of a timeless natural Gothic cathedral. In the beginning, they were only a mixture of coral and shells pressed on the seabed. Then they emerged; rain, wind, and time performed their work, producing the pointed forest hundreds of feet high that we admire today, a landscape ruled by boundless imagination. The landscape is unique in the world. The French realized its splendor in 1927, when in order to enhance it they transformed the Tsingy di Bemaraha area into an Integral Nature Reserve; in 1960, Unesco declared it a World Heritage Site. Here, everything seems to have taken its own path. Isolation has contributed to making 85% of the plant species endemic, while 11 species of lemur have taken up residence here: from the Milne-Edwards' sportive lemur (*Lepilemur edwardsi*, a smiling face and large eyes that would be the envy of a Japanese cartoon) to the rufous brown lemur (*Eulemur rufus*,

electrifying fur, ghostly gaze). Among the *tsingy*, the entire animal kingdom takes on dreamlike qualities.

You can meet little geckos and multicolored chameleons. If you look up to the sky, you catch the flight of the Madagascan fish eagle, the harrier or the little grebe. If you're lucky, you might also see the Madagascan white-browed owl.

You are accompanied by a guide in the nearly 270 square miles of the reserve. The simplest route can lead to a feeling of disorientation in 4 or 5 hours: standing among the canyons, in a real labyrinth, and then you ascend to experience the thrill of the void, almost ecstasy when confronted with the infinite shades of vegetation seen from above; or entering the grottoes in search of ancient presences, perhaps human. Another route, more suitable for the physically fit, leads you in six hours to savor the fear of a suspension bridge as you climb to the highest point for a glimpse of the horizon.

The highest level of adventure is to sleep in the park: in a few days' exploration, you can best tackle the Grand Tsingy, the route in the Broadway grotto that winds among pinnacles in the most bizarre shapes, tunnels, and limestone terraces. On the floor of the canyons with dense vegetation, humidity concentrates more heavily, and then thins as you climb toward the top and shrubs gradually become drier. It is here that you have the time to get to know the lemurs and be enchanted by their vitality.

ON LAKE BAIKAL, WHERE THE ICE IS BLUER

AS YOU VENTURE ACROSS THE SHEET OF ICE COVERING IT IN WINTER, YOUR EYES PENETRATE DOWN INTO THE DEPTHS OF THE DEEPEST AND MOST TRANSPARENT LAKE ON THE PLANET.

Your head spins. While you are walking on the enormous blue plain, on the transparent ice and its crevices, your eye focuses to a depth of several feet and your head begins to spin. It is a unique experience on the Earth, because Lake Baikal is the deepest and the clearest lake on earth. It is surrounded by mountain chains with peaks between 6,500 and 9,800 feet, woods on the lower slopes and fed by 366 tributaries, with a single majestic outflowing stream, the Angara.

86-87   The proud pinnacle of the island of Ogoy, surrounded by a sheet of ice on Lake Baikal. In summer, it is linked to the mainland by a ferry.

87   For the Buryats, the most numerous ethnic minority living in the region, Lake Baikal is "dalai nor" (sacred sea): according to legends, two evil demons live on the bottom of the lake.

88 top   The presence of this great body of water, which is surrounded by a chain of mountains and has 330 tributaries, mitigates the very low temperatures of the entire region.

88 bottom   A boy poses for the camera, while in the background a van crosses the lake as if it were a normal highway. The vehicles used are mainly old Soviet ones.

89   A camp at -22 °F requires tough, insulated equipment.

 ## ADVICE FOR TRAVELERS

WHEN TO GO In winter, from February to March, to enjoy the extraordinary transparency of the ice. In summer, from mid-June to mid-August, to travel the Great Baikal Trail around the lake.

HOW TO GET THERE It is a five-hour flight from Moscow to Irkutsk, on the southern shore. From here the train takes 34 hours to travel north to Severobajkal'sk. The reference point on the lake is Listvjanka.

WHAT YOU NEED High-altitude mountain clothing, a windproof jacket for polar temperatures, waterproof ski pants, thermal gloves and underwear, winter trekking boots, ice crampons, sunblock cream, a camera with good supply of reserve batteries.

DIFFICULTIES Ability to withstand low temperatures: at night they descend to -22 °F.

WEB SITES rusmania.com/practicalities/winter-lake-baikal-advice, waytorussia.net/Baikal, www.irkutsk-baikal.com, greatbaikaltrail.org/en

In winter, the great expanse of water is chilled by the Siberian cold, which creates a surreal landscape around it. From January until the end of April, the lake is covered with a layer of ice from 5 to 6.5 feet thick. It is safe not only for one of the most unusual treks on the planet or for lovers of winter sports – from skating to curling, to dog sledding – but also for motor vehicles. In fact, after the officers of the Russian ministry for emergencies have checked its solidity, at the end of January, road signs are installed on the frozen surface of the lake and Baikal can be used by cars and trucks – with special rules and safe routes – making it faster and easier to move between the towns along its shores.

The transparency that transforms Baikal into the largest, and most magical, skating rink in the world (395 miles long and on average 30 miles wide, at some points almost 50) is caused by a combination of various climatic and geological factors.

And also by the introduction of environmental rules in the nineteen-eighties, like prohibiting the lumber industry to float trunks downstream on the rivers, which was a source of pollution. In winter you cross the lake on ice skates or crampons to admire not only the frozen surface but also the world underneath: the extremely cold climate means little snow, leaving the ice clear.

The lake is 5,387 feet deep in the central part, a world record. Baikal contains the largest concentration of freshwater on the planet: 5,670 cubic miles (equivalent to the mass of water flowing annually in all the world's rivers), 80 per cent of Russia's water resources, and 20 per cent of the world's, excluding solar ice caps and high-altitude glaciers.

Because the percentage of oxygen in its crystalline waters is very high (a 75% saturated solution), life is possible even in its darkest depths, a unique situation.

In other lakes, microorganisms disappear below a depth of 980 feet because of the absence of oxygen. The richness in oxygen encourages extraordinary biological and endemic variety: in fact, many species prosper only here. It is an Eden of continuously evolving flora and fauna. Among the very high number of crustaceans, there are the numerous *Epischura baikalensis*, shrimps crucial for the fabulous transparency of the lake: they filter the water and leave it clean and limpid. The *Epischura* prospers in Baikal owing to the high concentration of oxygen, the low level of salinity and the low temperature of the water. There are 52 fish species, among which the *Comephorus baikalensis*, a transparent species without scales: At sundown it emerges from a depth of 1,600 feet to feed on plankton living on the surface, and then at first light it dives back into the depths because it cannot survive above 44 °F. There is also the omul (*Coregonus migratorius*), a kind of whitefish that for centuries has constituted the main food source of the Buriati people, of Mongol ethnicity, who live on the shores of the lake. However, Baikal's most representative species is the Baikal seal (*Pusa sibirica*), a small seal with a dark gray coat; it is at the top of the lake's food chain, and feeds on the fish it captures by digging holes into the ice on the lake. Although it was hunted for two centuries, this species is flourishing and its number is estimated at 75,000.

Among the grassy, often boggy, meadows and the low vegetation of the tundra, woods of birches, Arolla pines, larches, silver firs, Siberian pines, and Siberian cedars are home to 230 bird species, 146 of which nest here. To protect the migratory birds, a bird sanctuary has been created on the delta of the Selenga tributary: it is the best place for bird-watching. Other nature reserves protect elk and sable, which are present in the 14 million hectares of forests in the district of the lake, together with the East Siberian Brown Bear (*Ursus arctos collaris*), with very thick fur and standing 8 feet tall. These features led to Lake Baikal's being declared a Unesco World Heritage Site in 1996.

The summer begins at the end of June and finishes at the end of August with the first frosts. For hiking fans, it is the moment to travel the long path (Great Baikal Trail) which surrounds the lake.

The sarma is the wind that blows across its waters and shores and reaches the speed of 93 mph, but on the days that it does not blow, all the wonders described here are ready to surprise you.

90 The crystallized formations created by gas under the surface are in harmonious and original patterns.

91 top While a diver swims in the water of Baikal, a vehicle crosses its surface. Crossing the lake instead of going around it reduces times and distances considerably.

91 bottom Two tourists peer through the layer of ice to try to understand its mystery. Eastern Russia, remote and uncontaminated, has always attracted tourists seeking direct contact with nature.

KAMCHATKA: LAND, FIRE AND ICE

ONE OF THE LEAST POPULOUS REGIONS ON EARTH, THE MOST DYNAMIC GEOLOGICAL WORKSHOP ON THE PLANET, WHERE YOU CAN SPOT THE BROWN BEAR AMONG THE VOLCANOES AND GEYSERS.

With 414 glaciers, 160 volcanoes of which 29 are active, 14,000 rivers, 100,000 small and large glacial lakes, the Kamchatka is unique on the Earth, one of the most remote nature paradises. Here you can find total silence, encounter bears, and be immersed in pristine nature. It is a peninsula in the form of a crab's claw, as the Russian writer Viktor Erofeev described it, with a surface area of 184,000 square miles, 745 miles of which extend from the eastern extremity of Siberia into the Bering Sea.

92   A brown bear with seagulls on Lake Kuril, an excellent feeding ground for both.

92-93   The brown bear, a species of Siberian bear that competes with the polar bear for the title of largest land predator. This species is principally found in in Asia and North America.

▶▶ ADVICE FOR TRAVELERS

WHEN TO GO   The best period is from June to September, to avoid the most intense cold. The temperatures are around 59 °F; it is the rainiest region in Siberia, with heavy snowfall in winter in the mountain areas. Helicopter tours over the Valley of the Geysers and Lake Kuril last from July to October.

HOW TO GET THERE The capital Petropavlovsk-Kamčatskij can be reached by plane, more rapidly from Moscow with Russian airlines, or from Alaska. You can then rent a car in the city, preferably a 4X4.

WHAT YOU NEED Warm clothes (fleece sweater and long underwear if traveling in winter) and hiking boots, gloves, windbreaker, and sunglasses.

DIFFICULTIES Accessible to everyone, but good stamina is useful during the long excursions.

WEB SITES
www.en.pioneer-kamchatka.ru
kamchatka.org.ru/eng
www.travelkamchatka.com

It is a sulfurous universe, one of the most geologically active regions on the planet, with a mountain chain of volcanic origin 500 miles long, the greatest concentration of geysers in Eurasia and a myriad of hot water springs. Off the peninsula, the Kuril trench is 21 miles deep.

In Kamchatka the Euro-Asiatic and Pacific plates converge at a speed of 0.7 inches per year: the Oceanic plate formed of basaltic rocks rich in water, bends under the continental one. The result is a landscape of rough, extraordinary beauty,

the dream of every eco-tourist, a setting that combines such ecosystems as marshes with grass 10 feet high, Siberian taiga and Arctic tundra. A patchwork of craters, springs, waterfalls, boiling rivers, turquoise lakes, geysers 40 feet high, fumaroles, petrified birch woods, and eternally snowy peaks.

An unreal silence covers this wild region, with very low human presence (fewer than one inhabitant per square mile). In part this is due to the inhospitable climate, warmer than in continental Siberia

but with extremely long winters – it freezes from October to June – with temperatures dropping to a -40 °F and brief, hot summers, with daily temperatures reaching 95 °F, then dropping at night.

Until the mid-eighteenth century, when it was reached by a Russian exploration ship, the Kamchatka was inhabited only by occasional villages of fishermen and Siberian reindeer breeders, a people so "primitive" that the botanist Stepan Krašeninnikov, in his travel log, described them as "just one step above

photography, died here in 1996 in a bear attack.

The brown bear of the Kamchatka (*Ursus arctos beringianus*), the gigantic Siberian species which lives in these lands, is the nearest relative to the North American grizzly bear. Standing 9.8 feet high and weighing as much as 1,400 pounds, it rivals the polar bear for the title of largest terrestrial carnivore. In summer, it stores up more than 390 pounds of fat to withstand the long winter hibernation. It is an excellent swimmer, and the only animal capable of fighting off the Siberian tiger. It is no accident that it is considered the king of the 918 animal species in the Kamchatka. Between 15,000 and 30,000 brown bears live on the peninsula, the largest concentration in the world.

The best place to spot the bear is Lake Kuril, where at least 3,000 salmon – the bear's main prey – live and deposit their eggs. Lake Kuril – located on the tundra 125 miles south of the capital, almost at the southern point of the peninsula – can be reached in an hour on board one of the large Russian military helicopters. It is equipped with electrified bear-watching shelters. All the excursions are conducted safely, with an armed ranger. Even at a distance, it is thrilling to encounter a bear: the giant is immersed in the water, and with its paws it seizes the salmon with a great splash and then sinks its teeth into them.

the animals." They were a people who, apart from the scholar's Eurocentric judgment, lived in total symbiosis and harmony with the environment. The peninsula developed thanks to strategic military bases built during the Cold War, and today has just 334,000 inhabitants, almost totally concentrated in the capital, Petropavlovsk-Kamčatskij.

Kamchatka only has a few hundred miles of paved roads, so it is one of the most difficult regions to cross. It has been open to tourism since the 1990s. When

you visit it – by 4×4, in a helicopter flying over the range of volcanoes, or on an icebreaker following the spectacular coast – you feel as if you are an explorer at the mercy of a powerful nature and a hostile climate. It is a strong, deep feeling that contributes to the hypnotic beauty of the peninsula, considered a photographer's paradise. Sebastião Salgado immortalized it in his project *Genesis*, to discover the places where the world began. And Michio Hoshino, the most famous hunter of images of *ursidae* in the history of

94 top Fumaroles in the caldera of the Uzon volcano. Together with the caldera of the River Geysernaja, it is home to the most extensive geothermic field on the peninsula.

94 bottom An emerald green volcanic lake at the foot of the smoking plume of the Gorely volcano.

95 Brown bears fishing for salmon; however, their diet is mainly based on vegetation.

96-97 Large sockeye salmon shoals in Lake Kuril, where at least 3,000 salmon lay their eggs; salmon can even reach 15 pounds in weight.

97 The very brief moment of the capture. For brown bears, salmon are almost the sole source of animal proteins. Before hibernation, the bear goes through a phase of hyperphagia, frenetic feeding of up to 33 pounds per day. This assures reserves of fat to survive the long winter.

You also meet the brown bear in the Kronockij, a nature reserve created in 1934, situated a three-hour helicopter flight north of the capital. The park includes most of the geographic elements of the Kamchatka: tundra, a glacial lake, a river, the spectacular Valley of the Geysers (from the helicopter you can see very many bears, also mothers and cubs) with 26 boiling water jets, fumaroles, hot springs, a forest of dwarf birches, weeping willows and Swedish sorbus trees: the most representative flora in a peninsula where

1166 plant species have been cataloged: rhododendrons, chrysanthemums, wild garlic, and above all berries: blackberries, red currants, cranberries, honeysuckle, and gooseberries, together with lynches, foxes, sables, reindeer, wolves, seals, orcas, and 160 bird species, among which Steller's sea eagle, the largest in the world, with black and white plumage and a long yellow beak.

One negative point is that hunting is permitted for tourists, even if there are some limitations.

FISHING FOR THE SOCKEYE SALMON

The seas and rivers of the Kamchatka boast the world's greatest concentration of sockeye salmon (Oncorhynchus nerka), which can reach 3 feet in length and 15 pounds in weight. They are the most common food source for bears and eagles. Avacha Bay, just south of the capital, is one of the main places for salmon reproduction.

Every year, in July and August, two million salmon reaches these icy waters to celebrate their rite of love, reproduction, and death. A host of brown bears awaits them on the bank of the river where they deposit their eggs. The scenes of these giants seizing the salmon in their paws in the rivers are among the most dramatic spectacles of the Kamchatka.

MONGOLIA

IN THE FOOTSTEPS OF GENGHIS KHAN

HORSEBACK RIDING, SLEEPING IN TENTS
AND WATCHING THE NAADAM, THE OLYMPICS
OF THE STEPPE. AROUND YOU ARE THE MOUNTAINS
AND LAKES OF THE FAR NORTH, THE SURVIVING
MONASTERIES, THE NOMADS, THE GOBI DESERT
AND THE FOSSILS OF DINOSAURS.

Luigi Barzini Jr. has the best metaphor: "a meadow which has become a sea."
A plain that the journalist describes as "devoid of trees, bushes, houses; there's not
even a scrap of paper." Mongolia is a mystery: there is nothing, it is empty,
but it bewitches: with its deep valleys, turquoise lakes, silent dunes and an endless
green ocean. But this alone does not explain the secret.

98-99 The Gobi Desert, in the Altai Mountains, in the Gobi Gurvansaikhan National Park: camels grazing
near a ger, a typical nomad tent.

99 Walking in Khongoryn Els, with dunes extending for 372 square miles.

WHEN TO GO The trip to Mongolia is the most pleasant from May to the beginning of October, when the country is not in the grip of the cold, nature comes alive and nomadic life begins again. In the second week of July (always check the exact date) there is the great Naadam festival, for which you should book well ahead.

HOW TO GET THERE From Ulan Bator you travel in the interior by car or by plane. Once you reach the area of interest, don't forget a horseback itinerary.

WHAT YOU NEED The temperatures can fluctuate between +105 °F and -40 °F, so your clothing should vary. In general, don't forget comfortable shoes for hiking and technical equipment, above all for the winter, sun protection cream, basic medicines (be careful of ticks) and cash to change (credit cards are only accepted in the capital).

DIFFICULTIES For the trip, you need to be adaptive and have some stamina, especially for the long journeys, in a 4X4 or possibly on horseback or on foot.

WEB SITES
www.travelmongolia.org
www.mongolia.travel

100 top, bottom and 101 The simple life of a family of horse, goat, and camel breeders, at the foot of the Altai Mountains, in the Ômnôgov' Province.

102-103 Waterfall on the River Ulaan Tsutgalan, in the Orhon Valley, declared a Unesco World Heritage Site in 2004 given the cultural importance of nomadic pastoral traditions.

Mongolia is a nation five times the size of Western Europe, inhabited by three million people with very few paved roads. However, it has become a symbol of something else: adventure, nomadic life, freedom. Mongolia is essentially an experience: traveling on horseback on the steppe; adopting the tempo of a proud and rebellious people; being welcomed to a *ger*, a circular felt tent, to drink together a cup of *airak*, fermented mare's milk. To experience all this, you only need to drive a few hours east of Ulan Bator, the capital, to Hèntij, the heart of the

Mongolian nation. There, silence is the protagonist, the horizons infinite, and meetings with others so rare as to become precious moments. There is inevitably an invitation to share the tent, the mat, the milk, which follow words when their meaning is only a hypothesis, and we glance at each other curiously. Then you start the journey again, the mountains in the distance, steppe as far as the eye can see, sunsets etched into the sky, nothing for miles, stars for millions of light years. This is Mongolia.

The province of Hèntij is the birthplace

of the national myth, Genghis Khan. A few years ago, the *Washington Post* proclaimed him Man of the Millennium: he was born from the strength of a wolf and the grace of a deer, and in the thirteenth century he united the Mongol tribes in the greatest empire ever seen. It is him that the wrestlers of the Naadam address when, after defeating their opponent, they dance, miming the eagle, in their leather boots and short narrow-waisted jackets. The Naadam festival, not to be missed, "the Olympics of the Steppe" is held in Ulan Bator in July: three disciplines – wrestling, archery and horse racing – which are the sublimation of nomadic life, when they hunted and waged war on horseback. "And there are multicolored tents / and the children sing in the expanse / and the eager horses of the steppe prepare for the races."

Horses were celebrated by the poet Dashdorjyn Natsagdorj, and are everything for nomads: According to a Mongolian proverb ,"When a man is separated from his horse, what else can he do but die?"

Giovanni Pian del Carpine visited the court of Güyük Khan (he was the grandson of Genghis Khan) in 1246 in the then capital Karakorum. In his *Historia Mongalorum* he has left us a description of Mongol habits and customs, which testifies to how little their way of life has changed in eight centuries. Despite pressure from the historic Soviet to sedentarize the Mongols and eliminate the Buddhist religion, and despite cellphones and globalization, their strange way of riding and shooting an arrow at the same time, life in the *ger*, the close relationship with livestock, and the hospitality reserved for strangers, who are welcomed with a cup of *airak*, have never changed.

NOT ONLY STEPPE

On the Russian border, the north of Mongolia is dominated by the great Lake Khovsgol. When it is frozen, in the first days of March an ice festival is held with sleigh races and shamanic ceremonies; while on the Chinese and Kazakh border we find Altai, a remote land of deserts and snow-topped mountains that is the habitat of wolves and snow leopards, where in October the Kazak hunters are the protagonists of the festival of the Eagles. This changes in the southern part Mongolia to a dry, cold, and rocky landscape where the nomads on camels migrate through a land from which the dinosaur fossils of Bajanzag emerge (the best ones are preserved in the museum of natural history in the capital): it is the Gobi Desert, with the Khongoryn Els dunes, fairy tale canyons of the Yol Valley and a natural fortress of Tsagaan Suvarga, the "white stupa."

When you gaze at the endless horizon from the top of this canyon, you understand the words of the poet Buyannemekh, who was born in the Central Gobi: "Mongolia is too vast a land for the most powerful wings . . . ."

CHINA●

DANXIA, THE RAINBOW MOUNTAINS

THERE IS A PLACE IN CHINA WHERE
THE MAGIC OF THE RAINBOW DOES NOT ASSUME
THE FORM OF EVANESCENT ARCS IN THE SKY,
BUT OCCURS IN CRYSTALLINE FORM
IN TRULY MULTI-COLORED MOUNTAINS.

104   The ravines of the Danxia Geological Park, formed by the erosion of atmospheric agents.

104-105   The coloring of the mountains takes on different shades and intensities depending on the moment of the day. The colors are most splendid on the days following rain.

The first time you see them
you can hardly believe they're real:
the rainbow mountains of the Zhangye
Danxia National Geological Park
in China display colors and
combinations which are so lively that
they seem to be a creation painted
by a talented artist, rather than
a naturally occurring formation.

Layered streaks and unusual colors,
different shades of red, green, yellow,
orange, and blue give rise to unusual

looking geological formations
in sometimes astonishing forms
and combinations.

The enchanted landscape owes this
unusual coloring to deposits of red
sandstone, iron, and other minerals
from over 200 million years ago.
They create a true rainbow effect,
painted into the rock with chromatic
stratification recalling a layer cake.

Over time, the movement of
tectonic plates modeled these

chromatic sediments, creating bizarre
and marvelous mountain waves of
varied dimensions. Erosion by rain
and wind did the rest.

The most attractive and most visited
area of this geological park is the
central part, above 650 feet elevation.
It is known as Linze Danxia Scenic
Area, and is almost equidistant from
the cities of Zhangye, to the west,
and Linze, the county seat.

Whether you access the protected

WHEN TO GO The best period to visit the rainbow mountains is from June to September, when the weather is milder and alternating intense sun and occasional rain bring out the contrast in colors. Winter visits are not recommended, because of the winds and below-zero temperatures.

HOW TO GET THERE By plane: The nearest city is Zhangye, in the province of Gansu, which is connected with the larger city of Lanzhou by daily internal flights or a direct train. There is a bus line between the station of Zhangye and the park, taking about 15 minutes.

WHAT YOU NEED Enough drinking water, a jacket even in summer because temperatures drop considerably at the beginning and end of the day, comfortable shoes suitable for walking on the sand, sun protection cream, and a hat. A scarf or shawl is useful for protection from the wind.

DIFFICULTIES Medium-low. The park bus stops at every scenic point and it is possible to choose timing and effort according to energy and fitness level.

WEB SITES
www.topchinatravel.com
www.chinaexploration.com
www.travelchinaguide.com

area through the northern entrance or the western one, it is possible to move freely, but only on foot or by park bus. The buses reach the four main viewpoints. The first is near the park entrance, about 10 minutes on foot, and gives one of the most extensive views.

You reach the second by a ten-minute walk from the first area. However, you need to be physically fit because it is higher (about 20 minutes is necessary to reach it) and you need the stamina to climb the 666 steps. The third lookout requires less effort and enables you to admire all seven color shades. Because of its orientation, the fourth and last scenic area is the one most suitable for photos at dawn and sunset. Exploring it may require from two to four hours, according to your personal need to contemplate, absorb, and be immersed in the sublime landscape.

106 and 107 top and bottom The streaks of the mountains vary, depending on the different minerals making up the terrain and the rock formation, dating from the Cretaceous period. The park extends for around 190 square miles at an altitude of 5,900 feet.

THE LOST KINGDOM OF MUSTANG

IN A DISTANT FRAGMENT OF TIBETAN LAND,
TEN DAYS' TREKKING AT 13,000 FEET, WITHIN SIGHT
OF THE HIMALAYAN GIANTS: REDISCOVER THE
ENERGY OF CREATION AMONG ANCIENT TEMPLES
AND EXTRAORDINARY GEOLOGICAL FORMATIONS.

Once upon a time there was the Kingdom of Mustang. It was isolated from everything, with icy passes defending it and some of the highest mountains in the world acting as sentinels. Only caravan routes crossed it, used by merchants who traded grains and fabrics between Nepal and Tibet, but access to foreigners was prohibited. Very few foreigners had the privilege of visiting it; among them the writer Fosco Maraini, who described the capital, Lo Manthang, as "a jewel of ancient Tibet."

108-109 The village of Chuksang, at 9,500 feet, in the lowest section of the Kali Gandaki Valley; the pyramid of Nilgiri (23,100 feet) rises in the background. It is part of the Annapurna massif.

109 A Tibetan bridge crosses the River Kali Gandaki, one of the main watercourses in Nepal.

Mustang remained a hidden jewel until 1992, when it cautiously opened its frontiers to tourism. This decision never affected the charm of this land of adventure, a strip of desert plateau, within sight of the great glaciers. Here, you can still be totally immersed in nature and in Tibetan culture, far from traffic and airports. Only a few thousand visitors are admitted each year, to remote villages and frescoed temples, where it is easy to feel as the first explorers did, of a medieval world that has miraculously remained intact.

Right from the little airport of Jomsom, you turn your back on the contemporary world: it is a single runway, twenty minutes by air from Pokhara. This is where the plateau trekking begins: the first stage is Kagbeni, a village of mud houses at 9,000 feet, on the banks of the Kali Gandaki. It is this river, crossing the whole of Mustang, which is the great guiding line for trekking:

a tributary of the Ganges, its source lies 20,000 feet above and cuts an impressive canyon, between Annapurna (26,545 feet) and Dhaulagiri (11,014 feet); its basin consists of over a thousand glaciers and hundreds of glacial lakes.

Five days' trekking is needed to reach the capital, Lo Manthang, in a phantasmagorical desert landscape, fringed with far-off eternal snows. The path crosses high passes, from Mu La (13,681 feet) to Marang La

ADVICE FOR TRAVELERS

WHEN TO GO The best time for trekking in Mustang is before or after the monsoons, which last from May to September. The weather is sunny and stable especially in October and November. From December to March, the region is covered in snow, with very low temperatures.

HOW TO GET THERE There are air and land connections every day from Jomsom to Pokhara, Kathmandu. For trekking, it is better to use local guides, who are supplied by many operators in Kathmandu. The cost of the permit (50 dollars per day) is usually included in the package.

WHAT YOU NEED You need specific clothing for the climate in the high mountains, such as gloves and a hat, glacier glasses, barrier creams and strong hiking socks. It is useful to have a sleeping bag for a temperature of 23 °F.

DIFFICULTIES The paths are easy, but the stages are long and demanding. Great differences in level and passes at over 13,000 feet require adaptation to altitude. For those who do not like walking, horseback rides and 4x4 trips are organized.

WEB SITES
www.welcomenepal.com,
www.mustangtrekkinginnepal.com

(13,877 feet), where you breathe the rarefied air of the Himalayas.

It then touches ancient monasteries like Ghar Gompa, founded in the eighth century, and traditional villages like Geling, where brightly-colored stupas stand, and Ghami, with its very long prayer wall. The profoundly mystical atmosphere is linked to thrilling views: the yellow rock crags carved by erosion into spectacular organ-pipe formations plunge into the valley, onto the sparse oases of fields cultivated in terraces. Above it all are the clear sky and the icy profile of the high peaks of Annapurna and of Nilgiri Himal. Finally, Lo Manthang appears to nestle between rounded hills, at 12,000 feet, surrounded by gardens and by the quadrilateral of medieval walls, whose doors to the king's temples were locked every evening.

It is the highest capital in the world, and also the smallest, with fewer than

110 Ascending to Rohi La, at 13,126 feet, against the background of the arid rocks of Mustang. All hikes along the Kali Gandaki include passes above 13,120 feet.

111 top A brightly colored stupa, (small Buddhist temple), near Tsarang.

111 bottom A herd of goats at Tetang; the village, destroyed in the 1960s during the Chinese Cultural Revolution, is half an hour on foot from Chhusang.

112   The red tints of sculpted sandstone form the fantastical scenery at the foot of Dhakmar. The color of the rock, narrates the legend, is that of the ogre Ballmo's blood.

113   Tibetan prayer flags decorate a stupa in Ghami, one of the most characteristic villages found along the valley of the Kali Gandaki. The river, which rises over 19,600 feet in the heart of the Himalayas, crosses the entire kingdom of Mustang and sustains vegetable gardens around the villages, the only green element in the desert landscape.

one thousand inhabitants. Its alleys, between lime-washed houses, have never heard the sound of an engine, only of people's footsteps and horses' hooves. (In the past, horses were reserved for the members of the king's family.) The royal palace, of an imposing size with five floors, dominates the center; there are four main temples, all of them built between the fifteenth and eighteenth centuries.

The best time to visit is May, the end of the dry season celebrated with the Tiji festival, a centuries-old festival that represents the struggle between good and evil with dances and sumptuous costumes: it is a true privilege to attend.

You can return southward from the capital by other hiking paths which lead to temples, like the splendid Luri Gompa, at almost 13,000 feet, with frescoes in Newari style (from the valley of Kathmandu), and to a trek through high passes like the Cha Cho La (13,172 feet), from which you can enjoy a superb view of Dhaulagiri.

The last stage before you enter Jomsom is the sacred temple of Muktinath (12,171 feet). The pagoda containing the statue of Vishnu is tiny, but it is here, at the foot of the Himalayan giants, that Buddhists and Hindus together worship the cosmic forces ruling creation.

In the last twenty-five years modernity has sought to burst into the ancient kingdom of Mustang: the monarchy fell in 2008, together with that of Nepal (of which Mustang is a part) and completely disappeared in 2016 with the death of the last king, Jigme Palbar Bista. Until the end, the ex-sovereign had continued to grant audiences to all the foreigners who wished to meet him. Today, the little kingdom is besieged by asphalted roads, from the north and from the south: they are being built by both the Chinese and Nepalese governments. Despite the cost of the residence permit, the influx of visitors is growing, and itineraries for 4x4s are now open. In any case, it remains the ideal destination for trekkers in search of fragments of an ancient world and true oases of spirituality.

INDIA

THE LIVING BRIDGES OF MEGHALAYA

VEGETATION, WATERCOURSES AND WATERFALLS, IN ONE OF THE RAINIEST REGIONS IN THE WORLD: HERE, PEOPLE CROSS RIVERS BY WALKING ALONG THE AERIAL RUBBER-TREE ROOTS.

Meghalaya is one of the Seven Sister States in the northeast of India, on the Bangladesh border. The name encapsulates the main elements of this land: in fact, *megham* means "clouds" in Sanskrit , and *alayam* means "dwelling," and in the kingdom of clouds the sky is rarely seen. In one of the wettest areas of the world, contact with nature in the jungle, considered sacred by the local population, has an almost primordial quality. During the monsoon season, the watercourses from mountain to valley are impossible to cross on foot. Thus more than a century ago,

114 The bridges of aerial roots that link the villages of Meghalaya are able to withstand one of the Earth's most humid climates; about a third of the region is covered with subtropical forests, with semi-evergreen plants.

114-115 The Double Decker Living Roots Bridge, in the village of Nongriat, an extraordinary two-level bridge.

Trees are the earth's endless effort to speak to the listening heaven.

Rabindranath Tagore

 ## ADVICE FOR TRAVELERS

WHEN TO GO During the monsoon, between May and August, the state of Meghalaya experiences heavy rain. Although the roads are in good condition, it could be difficult to follow the paths. This area holds the world records for annual, monthly, and daily rainfall (472 inches of rain a year in the last half century, for example). It is therefore better to arrange the trek between September and April.

HOW TO GET THERE The city of Guwahati in the state of Assam is the largest hub from which you can reach the capital of Meghalaya, Shillong, in private or shared taxis; alternatively, you can rent a car at the airport or online. For the treks between the living bridges, the nearest town is Cherrapunjee, which can be reached in 2 hours by road from Shillong.

WHAT YOU NEED The weather is unpredictable but always very wet; ideally, you should wear light clothing that dries quickly, long pants, a light raincoat and anti-slip hiking shoes.

DIFFICULTIES Everyone can do the trek, apart from very small children and adults with reduced mobility.

WEB SITES tourism.gov.in, www.incredibleindia.org

the Khasi – one of the three indigenous ethnic groups inhabiting the forest –conceived a system that exploits the natural power of vegetation. By interweaving roots, which can take more than twenty years, they create root bridges extending from the two banks of the watercourses and meeting halfway.

The result is a living link, constructed by humans and modeled by nature, which takes advantage of the strong roots of the rubber fig plants (*Ficus elastica*) winding around the betel trunks. The living bridges show that nature is wiser than man: the roots do not rot, despite the continuous rainy climate, and in fact grow ever stronger with the passing years.

The most famous of these natural bridges is near Nongriat, a small village which can only be reached on foot from the nearby village of Tyrna. It is called Double Decker Living Roots Bridge

(or Jingkieng Nongriat), and is a spectacular two-level bridge across the River Umshiang. In order to reach it, you must face 3500 steps, with the help of local experts and guides, through very steep jungle terrain, with suspension bridges, luxuriant vegetation, and butterflies of a thousand colors, in about a 3-hour hike. You should yield to the temptation to bathe in one of the natural crystalline water pools along the way, so as to be immersed further in nature and feel the enchantment of the running water. To be even further amazed, you can continue your trek for about half a mile toward Rainbow Falls.

116 Two Khasi children, from one of the ethnic groups living in the Meghalaya jungle, cross the river by an ancient bridge built by skillful interweaving. In the background, some Khasi women wash clothes in the river.

117 The Ritymmen Bridge, more than 98 feet long, is the longest living bridge.

THE SEA LIGHTS UP

ON MOONLESS NIGHTS, THE SHORELINE IS LIT UP BY
A CONSTELLATION OF LUMINOUS BLUE PHOSPHORESCENT
POINTS AS IF A STARRY SKY HAD COME TO EARTH.

At first, you might think you were in the presence of alien creatures or that you had ended up on the set of the film *Life of Pi.*

Sometimes they arrive en masse like phosphorescence gelatin deposited on the beach. More often, there are isolated encounters following imperceptible changes: a wave breaking lightly on the beach, a foot moving the water. Sometimes they are fleeting moments, and then the magic disappears. Other times the phenomenon lasts, and in this case you should get into the water and let yourself be transformed into a Futurist sculpture.

Although it is brilliant, the phenomenon of bioluminescence is still unclear. Only recently have scientists discovered that the glowing of this particular plankton is aroused by stress. Understandably, the microscopic organisms interpret meeting the beach or a foreign body as a dangerous situation and begin to emit a cold light. The chemical substance producing the light is called "luciferin." Some creatures need a particular food or the presence of another creature, but in this particular type of plankton, called dinoflagellata, produces it spontaneously. It is a cold light generating very little heat. Up to this point it all seems very clear, if it weren't for other researchers who assure us that the light is due not to plankton, but to small crustaceans, ostracoda, strange predators of less than 1 mm that glow to attract their prey.

118 and 119   The monocellular organism that generates the bioluminescence phenomenon is really tiny: it has a rounded shape and measures from 200 to at most 2,000 micrometers.

▶▶ ADVICE FOR TRAVELERS

WHEN TO GO The best period to try to witness the phenomenon is between June and September.

HOW TO GET THERE Once you reach Malé international airport, local travel to the atolls is by internal flights, seaplane or motorboat, or a combination of the three.

WHAT YOU NEED Summer clothing, swimming suit, sun protection cream, and sunglasses. For night-time watching, don't forget a light waterproof jacket or warmer clothing.

DIFFICULTIES Accessible to everyone.

WEB SITES
www.visitmaldives.com
www.maldives.com
www.123maldives.com

◀◀

120-121 Millions of *Noctiluca scintillans* cover a beach on the island of Vaadhoo, in the north of the archipelago. The plankton inhabit eutrophic waters, rich in nourishment, whose temperatures never rise above 86 °F. The energy they release is accumulated by solar radiation.

Apart from the scientific debate, it is both thrilling and romantic to see this phenomenon. Moonless nights are ideal, during the hottest seasons. The electric blue points of this glow can be seen in the Mediterranean (Corsica and Sardinia), the Caribbean (Panama and Puerto Rico), Australia, Thailand, and the Philippines. But the Maldives is the territory that boasts the greatest continuity of sightings, because the Indian Ocean appears to be more densely populated with these creatures than other seas. In large areas of the ocean, these creatures can reach a considerable concentration, and when large numbers of them touch a lagoon, as in the case of coral atolls, the masses of plankton drawn by the current become trapped. In this way, the phenomenon can be enjoyed by those lucky enough to be on the right beach. The islands with the greatest number of sightings are Vaadhoo in the Raa atoll and also Dhuni Kolhu in the Baa atoll. Moreover, this infinite archipelago astride the Equator is 500 miles long and 93 miles wide. Geographers calculate the total number of islands as between 1300 and 13,000, depending on criteria: whether one counts the reef outcrops, associated islands, or sandbanks.

The government of the Republic of the Maldives has decreed that there are 1192 Islands, grouped into 26 natural atolls. Of these, 202 are inhabited (meaning with at least a village and a mosque), to which about a hundred island-resorts can be added. And there is no shortage of lagoons that can host bioluminescent creatures.

HOW AN ATOLL IS BORN

The natural process for creating an atoll is much more complex than you might think. An atoll is an island, which in general in this part of the world is little more than a sandbank, of different possible lengths, with a barrier surrounding it just above the water surface. Or it would be better to say the opposite, because the true atoll is primarily the coral barrier surrounding a "pool" of sea that may "contain" one or more islands or none. The same barrier can be formed partly by islands or sandbanks emerging, or simply by coral.

The Maldives, like many other archipelagoes of atolls, is the result of volcanoes rising from the ocean floor; at the end of the process, the atolls are flooded by water. The edges of the craters, (or what remains of them due to the incessant pressure of currents and waves) have been colonized by corals, algae, microscopic polyps, madrepores, and other sea creatures (not in order of appearance).

SAILING AMONG LOTUS FLOWERS

A PALETTE-FULL OF COLORS THAT PERHAPS
ONLY NATURE CAN GIVE US, AN EXPANSE
OF FLOATING VELVETY COROLLAS IN SHADES
FROM BABY PINK TO DARK MAGENTA.

Northeast Thailand, province of Udon Thani. The boat begins its tour
of the Red Lotus Sea, in the Kumphawapi Reserve, which combines a tropical
flower garden with the peace of a lake reflecting the clear sky; a universe studded
with flower species as far as the eye can see: small rafts moored on the banks,
water lilies, wild plants, tiny fish among the algae.

122 Lotus flower corollas, in full flower; early in the morning is the best time to admire them. In the Oriental
tradition, they are the symbol of purity: although their roots are in the mud, their petals are immaculate.

123 A typical boat sailing on the lake, which is just 3 feet deep.

 ADVICE FOR TRAVELERS

WHEN TO GO The best time is the cold season, with the maximum flowering period from the beginning of December to the end of February; January is always the best month: around mid-month, the Red Lotus Sea Festival takes place.

HOW TO GET THERE You reach the Red Lotus Sea from Udon Thani airport in about 50 minutes by car along Route 2. It is easier to go by taxi, as the direction signs are often only in Thai.

WHAT YOU NEED Light clothing, better if in natural fibers; it is rarely too cool, and a jacket for some winter evenings is enough. Comfortable shoes and insect repellent.

DIFFICULTIES The area is not served by public transportation; once you have arrived, the visit is suitable for everyone.

WEB SITES
www.tourismthailand.org

After ten minutes of pleasant, slow sailing, you see the horizon become rose-colored, almost as though you were suddenly situated at the entrance to a parallel microcosm, crossed only by the birds gliding over the boats. Once within sight of the lotus flowers, in a scene where silence reigns, the reaction is disarmingly appealing. The corollas appear on the silvery surface of the water, delicate yet haughty: they know they are beautiful.

In Oriental culture, the lotus is a sacred flower, linked to meditation, spiritual elevation, and perfection.

They stretch as far as the eye can see, infinite shades of white, pink, red, and fuchsia. Time seems to expand during the tour, while you are seated on large seats covered with straw mats, in anticipation of arriving in the best lookout to immortalize forever something unforgettable.

The boat tours last from 45 to 90 minutes, and in the hottest hours a canopy protects the passengers from the sun. Around you, various islands seem to fluctuate as tourists pass. Statues of Buddha, sanctuaries, and pagodas look on, silent guardians of that unexpected fairytale world.

Dawn, when the corollas open, perfectly accompanies this extraordinary beauty. To seize the perfect moment, the contact, tours should be organized between six in the morning and midday.

124 Lotus flowers are gathered and used not only for decorative purposes, but also as an ingredient of various Asian dishes.

125 top Fishing on the lake takes place with traditional nets. Often they are crammed full of pangasius, a bony freshwater fish very common in Thailand.

125 bottom The Kumphawadpi reserve is home to numerous bird species, among which the wading bird.

VIET NAM

A JOURNEY THROUGH TIME

NATURE AS IT WAS 3 MILLION YEARS AGO:
UNDERGROUND RIVERS TO FORD, AMID JUNGLE
AND FERN FORESTS, AND NATURAL CONCRETIONS
TO CLIMB OVER, IN A VIETNAMESE GROTTO.

As soon as you set foot in the Son Doong grotto, you find yourself in a surreal, enchanted setting. Massive stalactites, some even 230 feet high, hang down, and imposing stalagmites rise from the ground; meanwhile, a fresh breeze, created by the special microclimate, envelopes like a caress, presaging the magic of the almost unreal subterranean jungle that emerges from the heart of the grotto. Enormous natural skylights, created by collapses of the ceiling about 300,000 years ago, allow light and

126-127 Hikers in the Son Doong grotto, illuminated by the sun's vertical rays. The first to venture into this natural labyrinth were British explorers led by the speleologist Howard Limbert.

127 A narrow passage between the cavities in the Hang En grotto. It is called the grotto of the swifts because many of them usually build their nests within it.

water to penetrate. Together with the watercourses, which cross the cave, sculpting the rocks into terracing and encouraging the proliferation of dense vegetation, there is a fascinating subterranean ecosystem comprised of ferns and varied wild flora. It is inhabited by snakes and monkeys, including the rare species the Hatinh langur (*Trachypithecus hatinhensis*), numerous winged animals, flying foxes, and tigers in the most isolated areas.

Clouds and fog banks, rain, thunderstorms, and waterfalls modify the illumination and atmosphere: dark tunnels and beaches bright with reflections, transparency, and shafts of dazzling light. The great spaces of the grotto are different at every hour of the day. Fossils dating from one million years ago, slippery calcium carbonate walls, and cave pearls in the dry pools co-exist in what is considered to be the largest cave in the world. It is 5.6 miles long, in places 300 feet high, and in some sections as much as 650 feet wide. It is spacious enough to hold a Boeing 747.

As you walk through the undergrowth, you seem to be moving through a piece of Amazonia transplanted into an enormous movie studio. It is stunning to think that all of this is real. The grotto of Son Doong, created by an underground river, is situated in the heart of the Phong Nha-Ke Bang National Park, a complex of over 300 caves and grottoes in one of the largest calcareous regions in the world, in the central-Vietnamese province of Quang Bình. It was discovered by chance by a local farmer in 1991, explored by team of professional speleologists in 2009, and opened to the public in 2013, but only to a limited number of visitors. The adrenaline-filled adventure includes hiking in the jungle, assisted rope climbing sections, and crossing underground watercourses. Experience suggests three nights to explore its vastness. You give up comfort, but not the privilege of sleeping within thousand-year-old walls, under a roof of billions of stars.

128 Speleological expeditions have counted 150 grottoes and 87 miles of tunnels; the passage of light enables vegetation to grow even in the darkest areas.

129 It is dinnertime in the only authorized rest area in the Hang En grotto.

IN THE KINGDOM
OF BIODIVERSITY

INFINITE ECOSYSTEMS, THOUSANDS OF TREE
SPECIES, BIZARRE FAUNA AND THE LARGEST FLOWER
ON EARTH: THIS IS THE TREASURE OF THE MULU
NATIONAL PARK, THE CHAMPION OF BIODIVERSITY.

It is no accident that it is called "the Garden of Eden": just consider that it contains
eight types of equatorial forest with thousands of plant species; or that a hectare
of its old-growth rain forest is home to a greater variety of plants than all of North
America; or that more than a thousand species of insect live in a single tree.

131 Sandstone spires emerge from the hot, humid jungle. Sharp and pointed, they can be up to 130 feet high.

130-131 A suspension bridge in the rainforest. Two thirds of Sarawak, the Malaysian region containing in
the Mulu National Park, is covered by rainforests.

WHEN TO GO The best period is from June to September. The monsoon is from December to March, but it rains all through the year with continuous torrid heat and extremely high humidity levels.

HOW TO GET THERE You can reach The Mulu National Park by plane: daily flights take off from Miri, and four flights per week leave from Kuching and Kota Kinabalu. The excursions in the park leave from the park offices; they are on foot or by boat, and always require a guide. You can only move independently on foot around the base and in the nearby resort.

WHAT YOU NEED Light outdoor clothing, long pants, hiking shoes, swimming suit, insect repellent suitable for the jungle, binoculars to watch the animals.

DIFFICULTIES Climate conditions can be crucial because of the high level of humidity; the visitor experience can be chosen on the basis of agility and physical fitness.

WEB SITES
mulupark.com
www.forestry.sarawak.gov.my
www.malaysia.travel

The roof of branches and lianas that covers the jungle hosts the most diverse array of animals: orangutans, gibbons, proboscis monkeys, bearded capuchin monkeys, lorises (minute nocturnal tree-living primates), eight varieties of hornbill, leaping lizards, monitor lizards, squirrels, frogs, and spiders so large that they can feed on birds. The protected area is a concentration of unparalleled records and unique natural phenomena.

Two thirds of the Park (2,908 square miles) is in the region of Sarawak, two thirds of which in turn is covered by forest, irrigated by a thousand watercourses. To reach Mulu from Kuching, the capital of Sarawak, the plane flies for two hours over an intricate humid forest, veined with winding, swollen rivers.

The surprises seem to end here, but the greatest attraction of the park has yet to appear. It is the network of caves, the most important Kars formation in the tropical regions. Be prepared for a journey under the Earth's surface, full of surprises, a natural amusement park for those not afraid to walk in a sunless world. Some grottoes can be reached from the park base in a pirogue or by walking along wooden gangways between towering

trees, marked by plates as in a botanical garden. This concentration of grottoes reveals a geological history of a million and a half years, a particular morphology alternating sandstone chambers and spires: the park is dominated by Gunung Mulu, a giant pinnacle 7,800 feet high.

There is a long series of caves, of which Deer Cave is the best known. The most spectacular are the contiguous Wind Cave and Clear Water Cave: you reach them in an hour by pirogue on the River Mulu and visit them thanks to a metal stair network which forms a gymkhana between stalactites and stalagmites.

Wonderment triumphs in your visit to the Deer Cave, about 2.5 miles on foot. It is a chamber with a double entrance, 2,600 feet long and 416 feet high, illuminated by great natural windows and inhabited by two million bats which, shortly before sunset, leave the cave in a continuous curved column, darkening the sky for an hour. Also within the cave

132 Inside the Deer Cave, whose geological formation dates from a million and a half years ago.

133 A partly navigable subterranean river runs through the Clearwater Cave, which extends for 66 miles.

live millions of swifts of four different species; they make edible nests (for five centuries they have been used in traditional medicine). Immediately afterward, there is the smaller Langs Cave, where the bats are easier to observe and small white blind shrimps, fully adapted to the darkness of the grotto, swim in the pools.

Clear Water Cave is the longest system in Southeast Asia, and through it flows the Melinau, a navigable underground river, which can also be impetuous and violent. Yet you would not say this once you leave the cave, where you can have a fresh swim in the deep pool it feeds. From here, you can reach the park area, stop to take lunch and breathe with the forest.

The boldest can venture even further, forging ahead to the grotto "of the origins" in groups of twelve by a brief boat journey and a walk. Cave crickets, bright-eyed spiders, and snakes with blue scales await you. But a park guide will always be there to show the way.

The park is studded with natural wonders. It is the second habitat for biodiversity after Amazonia, and the first for geological uniqueness with the greatest network of caves, but also with its truly extraordinary animal and plant diversity. Animals, plants, flowers, and insects: from orchids to termites, from deer the size of a cat to carnivorous plants. All this has placed the Mulu National Park among the Unesco World Heritage Sites for bio-diversity, geo-morphological uniqueness, and beauty of nature.

THE PENAN, THE ORIGINAL INHABITANTS

Halfway between the park base and Clear Water, you find a Penan village on the banks of the river. It is the most primitive ethnicity in Borneo, reduced to fewer than 4,000 individuals with an uncertain future. The Penan are one of the last hunter-gatherer nomadic peoples who live in symbiosis with the forest, do not practice agriculture and do not recognize private ownership of land. They have always lived in makeshift shelters of leafy branches beside forests of sago, a palm from the pith of which they derive flour. They spend two weeks at the most in the same place, and then continue moving and hunting–with the help of poisonous arrows shot from blow-tubes–such animals as deer, monkeys, clouded leopards, small black bears, and above all bearded boar - a wild species (Sus barbatus) with a thick beard that swims ably in the rivers of the park. On the Sarawak side of the park live the Iban and Orang Ulu, who are much more integrated and interested in trading with visitors.

JAPAN

ON THE PATHS OF THE CHERRY BLOSSOM

THIRTY THOUSAND TREES IN BLOSSOM
RAINING PINK PETALS THAT DANCE THEIR WAY
TO THE GROUND. THIS IS HOW SPRING
IS WELCOMED ON MOUNT YOSHINO.

The cherry blossom is anticipated, almost venerated, and with a theatrical quality other natural events do not possess: the blossoming of the cherry trees in Japan is something magical that is repeated every year between the end of March and the early days of May. *Hanami* – which in Japanese literally means "watching flowers" – is not limited to the contemplation of the ephemeral, intense beauty of the cherry tree crowns blown by the wind, but is rather a collective rite, a moment of celebration to usher in the season of rebirth with walks and picnics immersed nature.

136   An explosion of buds of 200 different varieties on Mount Yoshino, in the Nara Prefecture.

136-137   The residential district of Meguro, in Tokyo, at the most longed-for moment of the year: spring.

ADVICE FOR TRAVELERS

WHEN TO GO The days of cherry blossom vary from year to year, but the dates are announced in detailed forecasts, also online. The best period runs from the end of March to the end of April.

HOW TO GET THERE To see cherry blossom on Mount Yoshino, the closest station is Yoshinoyama on the Kintetsu Yoshino line. It takes about one and a half hours from the stations of Osaka and Kyoto. Cars park on the outskirts and there is a shuttle bus to the destination.

WHAT YOU NEED Comfortable shoes, a raincoat (just in case), and a picnic blanket. For women, you can immerse yourself in the Japanese culture and wear a kimono, as many women do: they have their photographs taken under the cherry trees in their best robe.

DIFFICULTIES You can choose longer or shorter routes on the mountain. The less fit can arrive at Yoshinoyama station on the mountain by the Senbonzakura funicular, while those with more energy can reach the top of the mountain in 5 miles.

WEB SITES
www.yoshinoyama-sakura.jp/english
www.town.yoshino.nara.jp/kanko-event/kanouki/kaika/
www.jnto.go.jp/sakura/eng/index.php

Maybe you don't have the time to repeat Will Ferguson's feat in *Hitching Rides with Buddha*, following the line of the blossoming of the *sakura* (*Prunus serrulata*) – from the late season in Sapporo, in the north, to the gardens of Kagoshima, among the southernmost cities. But here is still a place in the center of Nara Prefecture that presents the spectacle of 30,000 trees in blossom. This is Mount Yoshino, which for centuries has been considered one of the favorite places for walking among the petals, which gently float down, blown by the wind as if in slow motion.

It is said that the first trees were planted on its slopes more than 1300 years ago. Still today, it is home to more than 200 different varieties of cherry, blossoming at different times according to the four areas into which the mountain is subdivided, from the base to the summit. This allows the visitor to enjoy the blossom for almost a whole month. The cherry trees are also illuminated at night, and can be admired at any time, with ever-changing shades.

You can reach the city of Yoshino by funicular, or walk up a steep slope in about two hours: It is dotted with stalls for souvenirs and food, which is always wrapped in pink. There are temples, sanctuaries and lookout points along the way. But to enjoy fully the mystical atmosphere and not to miss a moment of the fragile beauty of the *sakura* in blossom, you should continue along the path to the summit of Mount Yoshino, accompanied by the song of birds and the melody of the wind through the branches.

138 The Nyoirinji temple, on Mount Yoshino, surrounded by trees in blossom. The beginning of spring marks the start of fertility and harvest celebrations for the Shinto religion.

139 Even if it is among the most difficult to reach, Mount Yoshino remains a favorite place for *hanami*.

THE POETRY OF THE FIREFLIES

THE ENCHANTMENT OF COUNTLESS INTERMITTENT LIGHTS
IN THE SILENCE OF THE JAPANESE WOODS, A SURREAL SPECTACLE
REPEATED EACH YEAR WITH THE ARRIVAL OF SUMMER.

You need: patient expectation, the silence of the Motosu Hotaru Park and the dark nights of early summer. Then the magic comes, transforming the forest into an enchanted place. Far from the lights of the city, among the dense, high, thin-trunked bamboo trees, appears the ever-moving glow of countless fireflies able to transport the observer into a timeless fairy tale. Their fluttering illuminates the darkness and announces the beginning of summer.

At one time *hotaru-gari* (firefly hunting) was common in Japan. Today, to safeguard this spectacle, only contemplation is allowed: it is cultivated almost religiously. The ritual enables you to approach nature softly, to connect symbiotically, and then to abandon yourself and be open to surprises.

The park in the Gifu Prefecture is not the only place to contemplate this phenomenon: there are woods and paddy fields, sometimes even a large garden or a city park, but they have common features: they are silent, close to sources of clean water, and with little light pollution. Avoiding the neon lights of Tokyo, they find small oases in the city, like the Hotel Chinzanso, the very central Fureai di Shibuya botanical gardens or the Seichi Park inside Yomiuri Land, the largest amusement park in the area, 25 minutes by train from the city.

Other places recommended are the Tsukiyono Firefly Village in Minakami, a town in Gunma Prefecture, and the Roman-no Mori Kyowakoku park in Chiba Prefecture.

140 The fireflies' courting rite lights up summer nights in Shikoku Forest, far from the city lights.

141 Photographing fireflies means letting them form long fluorescent trails in the image.

If it were not for our concept of weights and measures, we should stand in reverent admiration of the firefly as we do before the sun.

Kahlil Gibran

ADVICE FOR TRAVELERS

WHEN TO GO In May and June, in the Japanese rainy season.

HOW TO GET THERE The nearest airport to Motosu Hotaru Park is Nagoya, about an hour's journey on main roads.

WHAT YOU NEED Spring/fall clothing and something warmer for the humid nights. If you love photography, don't forget a tripod for long exposures.

DIFFICULTIES None, apart from having the patience to wait for the phenomenon to occur, normally between 7.30 p.m. and 9 p.m. from the end of May through June.

WEB SITES
www.japan.travel/en

The arrival of the fireflies coincides with the beginning of the Japanese rainy season. The extremely humid air creates the ideal meteorological conditions for the proliferation of these delicate creatures, which light up the darkness like stars fallen to earth.

The light emission is part of the courtship fireflies' ritual: the males use bioluminescence to attract the females, which emit light at different rhythms. The general effect is of fireflies painting love letters in the air with fluorescent brushstrokes. Humans just have to sit back and contemplate the splendor.

142 Firefly males have a longer and slimmer body than the females and can fly higher.

143 The bridge over the river Taguchigawa at Aridagawa, in the Wakayama Prefecture, from which you can admire this spectacle of light. These fireflies only live where the water is clean.

DIP INTO THE FOREST

ASCENDING THE SLOPES OF THE VOLCANO YAKEDAKE, AND
ALLOWING YOURSELF TO BE OVERWHELMED BY THE VEGETATION.
WITH *SHINRIN-YOKU* THE FOREST IS TRANSFORMED IN AN
EXERCISE OF CONTEMPLATION AND ACCEPTANCE.

The philosopher and samurai Ekken Kaibara used to say that there were thunderstorms so majestic that one had to sit quietly and welcome them. The deep bond between humankind and nature has always permeated the Japanese sensibility. Japan is a delicate but violent land where grace and beauty coexist with strength and ferocity.

Today, most Japanese live in megalopolises where access to nature is difficult. *Shinrin-yoku*, also known as "forest bathing," is a therapeutic practice that consists in abandoning oneself to the beneficial power of the forest to combat the stress of everyday life. The theory of this exercise dates from 1982, but its roots lie in the connection of Shintoism, Buddhism, and Japanese culture with landscape. The Japanese forestry authority has identified about 60 of these itineraries: a true nature retreat in which one merges with the forest, listens to the sound of a stream or is lost in touching the knotty trunk of a tree. Forest bathing is a spiritual exercise requiring one to dare to abandon daily life. It is said that the benefits of this practice include lower blood pressure, reduction of cortisol, higher immunity to disease, increased energy and reduced depression and anxiety. In *Shinrin-yoku*, there is nothing to conquer. You need to leave behind your pedometers, telephones, and cameras.

144 Path on the Kamikochi plateau extending for about 15 kilometers in the valley of the River Azusa. In 1915, the Yakedake volcano erupted violently, creating a landslide that blocked the course of the river, giving rise to a small lake, Lake Taisho.

145 The river Azusa flows through vegetation, not far from Kamikochi, the hikers' destination.

146 Before the advent of European climbers and hikers, these places were often principally used by monks in search of an ascetic life. The high vertical tree trunks resemble temple columns.

147 When autumn comes, the forest begins to turn yellow, giving rise to a technicolor spectacle. It brings humans closer to the ephemeral beauty of nature.

 ## ADVICE FOR TRAVELERS

WHEN TO GO You can do the excursion easily from June to the beginning of November.

HOW TO GET THERE From Matsumoto train station (Japan Rail Shinonoi Line), take the Kamikochi line as far as Shinshimashima. Take the Kamikochi bus and get off at the Taisho-ike stop.

WHAT YOU NEED It is advisable to take layered clothing, a windproof jacket, hiking shoes, and a hat.

DIFFICULTIES The excursion is of medium difficulty. The entire route from the starting point up to the peak of the volcano is a 5-6 hour walk, there and back, with a difference in level of 3,100 feet. Those who suffer from dizziness are advised to pause halfway.

WEB SITES www.kamikochi.org, www.go-nagano.net, www.visitmatsumoto.com

The trail in the forest covering the slopes of the active volcano Yakedake, literally "the mountain that burns," is easy to cover between June and November. It starts from a plateau 4,900 feet above sea level, in the Chūbu-Sangaku National Park located in the Hida Mountains, the Northern Alps between the prefectures of Nagano and Gifu, along the banks of the River Azusa. The starting point is Lake Taisho, which can be reached by bus or car from Matsumoto or Takayama. From here, you enter the forest, and then climb up to the volcano's smoking crater, at 8,000 feet above sea level. The road

runs along the river bank, and then crosses the bridges of Tashiro-bashi and Hotaka-bashi to the other side, where the forest and the mountain stand out. The pristine waters of the river and Lake Taisho mirror the Japanese birches and larches blackened by the latest eruption of the volcano, creating an evocative, still, silent landscape. Past the fork for Mount Nishihotaka, you turn left and after about ten minutes' walk you are in the heart of the forest. The silence of the lake underlies the noise of the wind moving the crowns of the trees. The light penetrates the leaves, penetrating the forest and transforming it into a sacred cathedral. The damp earth, teeming with life, is a sea of moss that climbs up the trunks. The network of roots, as strong as giant serpents, forms pools that are transformed into lakes for frogs, snakes, and insects. The bright undergrowth rustles under the bodies of the Japanese macaques (*Macaca fuscata*) hiding there. The forest takes over

from humans and the outside world is silenced. Beyond the river, everything has disappeared. Only the present exists. After about 45 minutes' walk, the road begins to ascend. An iron and wooden bridge takes you into an area of wild flowers and shrubs. Here a small shelter sells water and noodles in packets. In the distance, you can see the rocky summit of the volcano emitting smoke. Past the shelter on the left, the path continues on rock and moss. The first gas fumaroles split the stone. From this point, if it is not covered by clouds, you can reach the summit of the volcano, in whose crater there is a small, frozen lake. It is an hour and a half's walk, and you should be careful to follow the signs on the rocks.

Shinrin-yoku means observing the forest, surrendering to its beneficial power, welcoming it within oneself and letting oneself be transported, for once, outside oneself. Forget everything except the present.

CANADA

FANTASTIC LIGHTS IN THE NORTH

IN THE FAR-NORTH REGION OF YUKON, HUNTING AURORA BOREALIS, THE MAGIC OF THE NORTHERN NIGHTS. THE ENCHANTMENT THAT THAWS THE ICE, A SIGN AND PROMISE OF FERTILITY.

The Klondike of Scrooge McDuck, the White Pass, the gate of ice and snow separating newcomers from the glittering promises of the most famous gold rush, Dawson City and the atmosphere of White Fang, the legendary Dempster Highway, the unpaved road that like an arrow points toward the far north, crossing some of the most majestic scenery in Canada; and finally Whitehorse, the capital with a frontier feeling. Above you, an endless sky, which acts as a backdrop for the dance of the Northern Lights.

148 An igloo, the historic dwelling of the Inuit people, built using blocks of snow placed in concentric circles, is illuminated by the Aurora Borealis.

148-149 The Aurora Borealis, which has always been associated by the Inuit with the celestial dance of spirits, seen from the icy region of Nunavut.

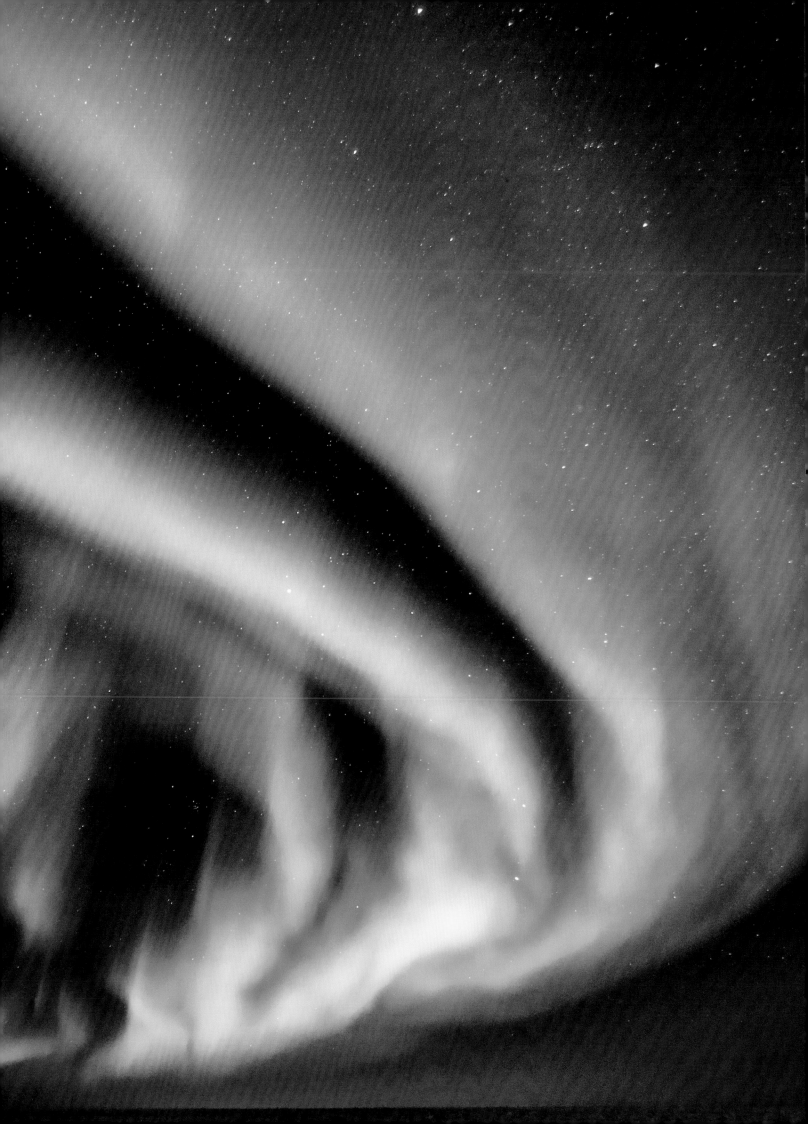

150 The phenomenon of the Aurora, which can create a thrilling atmosphere, was explained for the first time by the Norwegian physicist Kristian Birkeland at the end of the 19th century; but it was Galileo who gave it the name we know today.

151 The Aurora over Lake Superior; it is tinged with blue when the solar particles come into contact with nitrogen atoms instead of oxygen atoms.

 ## ADVICE FOR TRAVELERS

WHEN TO GO The entire year, but to observe the Aurora the best period is from October to April.

HOW TO GET THERE By plane as far as Whitehorse, then by rental car, preferably a 4X4.

WHAT YOU NEED Warm winter clothing as for an expedition, gloves and hat; spare batteries for photographic equipment.

DIFFICULTIES The trip is not for everyone. In particular, in winter it is essential to have experience driving on ice and snow, and familiarity with the intense cold and wild nature of northern regions.

WEB SITES www.travelcanada.ca, www.dempsterhighway.com, www.travelyukon.com, www.naturetoursyukon.com/winter-tours-yukon

The Yukon is one of the wildest regions of Canada, with fewer than 30,000 inhabitants in an area much greater than Arizona, where you find clear skies and little or no light pollution. These are the two main factors making the Yukon an ideal destination for those wishing to admire the Northern Lights.

It is not necessary to wait for the heart of the arctic winter, with its extreme temperatures. In Whitehorse, the high temperature in winter does not exceed 23 °F, with low temperatures around -13. Even in the mid-seasons like October or April, when the hours of light and darkness are more or less the same, it is possible to enjoy the spectacle provided by the sky while also enjoying what the

area can offer in the daytime. Obviously to see the Lights you need a clear sky, to stay awake at night, to have suitable equipment for the intense cold, and to move away from the city. The dance of the Aurora Borealis in the winter sky, which is sometimes sensual and sometimes convoluted, enchants everyone. Fleeting apparitions, sometimes persistent, often amazing: in any case, they create deep emotions and memories that do not fade in time. In reality, the phenomenon occurs in both the polar regions over the entire year.

A forest begins just outside Whitehorse, with chocolate-colored hills, and turquoise or emerald lakes as far as Dawson

City, 330 miles away. The road follows the course of the River Yukon, looks over its canyons, and touches the rapids. The darkest nights are found further north, along the Dempster Highway linking Dawson City with the Inuit of the North-West Territories.

Dawson City is left over from the mythical gold rush, which from 1896 onward sent half the world crazy. Bankers, poor men and fathers of families abandoned everything to rush to this remote and inhospitable corner of the world. Many died, others made their fortunes, most returned home with some stories to tell and lighter pockets: Jack London was one of these.

The city is still linked to the past, with muddy streets, rather lopsided wooden buildings and plays relating the golden age. Gold is still extracted, even if in smaller quantities and with less rudimentary methods. The best place near Dawson City to see the Aurora is Midnight Dome, a spectacular viewpoint along the Yukon River.

The Dempster Highway begins here, 25 miles west of the town, along the North Klondike Highway, 460 miles of unpaved road linking the Yukon to the furthest northern border through endless landscapes. The road symbolizes the journey to the far north, and offers rarefied air, an ever-changing sky, distant horizons and, above all, solitude. As it moves toward the Arctic, the Dempster Highway is transformed in every season: the northern summer, with melted ice, mud and mosquitoes; autumn with its explosion of colors and the nights lengthening with the first sighting of the Aurora; the winter with total silence, the roads of ice and snow, the sky transformed into a glittering stage; the brief spring, when the tundra is covered with flowers.

One last site: the Eagle Plains, one hour from the Arctic Circle, are one of the best places in Canada to observe the Aurora and star-studded skies, owing to the total absence of light pollution and clear air.

152-153   The reflection of the Aurora on the surface of the Heart River, in Alberta. The motto of the village of Nampa, not far from the river, is "a place near the heart," because of the peace on its banks, which the Aurora makes truly special.

CANADA

ENCOUNTER WITH THE NARWHAL IN BAFFIN BAY

IN SEARCH OF THE UNICORN OF THE SEA,
A MYSTERIOUS CETACEAN WITH A LONG TUSK,
THAT LIVES IN ARCTIC WATERS. SHY AND SOLITARY,
IT IS THE DREAM OF MANY WHALE WATCHERS.

A long, spiral tusk appears from the waves followed by the body of a small whale that leaps like a dolphin and then dives down into the depths. It is the narwhal (*Monodon monoceros*), the sea unicorn that lives in Baffin Bay, one of the remotest places in the Arctic, between Baffin Island – in Nunavut, the Inuit region of northern Canada – and Greenland. The area of the bay is 266,000 square miles, the same area of Texas, and its average depth is 2,800 feet.

154-155 A pod of narwhals emerges to breathe in a fracture of the pack ice in Baffin Bay: these mammals can stay submerged for up to 20 minutes.

155 Although it lives in extreme areas, the narwhal is ever more threatened by human activity and climate changes, which endanger its ecosystem.

156 top An explorers' camp in the Sirmilik National Park, which in the Inuktitut language means "place of glaciers": Inuit life and culture are rich in this protected area.

156 bottom The name "narwhal" seems to derive from the Ancient Norwegian *narhval*, "whale corpse," because of its pale coloring.

157 The long tooth that has made the narwhal an almost mythical creature is a prerogative of adult males. Many hypotheses have been formulated about its purpose.

 ## ADVICE FOR TRAVELERS

WHEN TO GO Baffin Bay is only accessible in July and August: it is covered with ice in winter, and in the mid-seasons it is full of giant icebergs, so navigation in icebreakers is limited to the summer.

HOW TO GET THERE In Nunavut there are no roads or railways. There are daily flights for the region of Qikiqtaaluk (weather permitting) from Ottawa and Montreal. There are also Air Greenland helicopter services from Nuuk, the capital of Greenland. The simplest way to visit Baffin Bay is an icebreaker cruise organized by a specialist company.

WHAT YOU NEED Clothing for a polar expedition. Knee-high rubber boots, hiking shoes on the ice, windproof jacket for polar temperatures, waterproof rain pants, fleece, gloves, cap, thermal underwear, and sunglasses.

DIFFICULTIES Accessible to everyone.

WEB SITES www.destinationcanada.com, www.nunavuttourism.com

The narwhal is a fascinating animal, starting from its appearance. The presence of a long tusk, to be precise a tooth, is rare, perhaps unique, among related animals. It is not used to hunt or spear its prey, but it is a sensory organ enhanced by 10 million nerve endings. It can reach up to 10 feet in length and weigh 22 pounds. The most recent hypotheses describe it as a source of information *par excellence* on temperature, salinity, and water pressure. In winter, it is fundamental for identifying holes in the ice through which the narwhal emerges to breathe. In ancient times, the tusk was thought to have powerful antidotal properties: drinking from a narwhal beaker made one immortal, and they were used as gifts between sovereigns.

It is easy to spot them around the Bylot Island Migratory Bird Sanctuary, home to over 200,000 migratory species per year, in the Sirmilik National Park: they never swim alone, and often move in groups of around fifteen. Sometimes they form groups of hundreds, so that the magic of the encounter is magnified. Small sand-gray waves appear on the surface of the icy water: they are the dorsal

areas of these primitive mammals which follow one another at regular intervals. The cruises skirt the northeastern coast of Baffin Island, from south to north, and offer kayak tours that enable you to come still closer to the shore. It is thrilling to sail to the limits of the ice floes, in the dazzling white Arctic landscape, among the animals that in summer return to play in the waves. And the long unicorn's "sword" that suddenly emerges beside the boat is an unpredictable and unforgettable image. It is a meeting with the fantastical animals of fairy tales.

The narwhal shares the waters of Baffin Bay with the beluga whale (*Delphinapterus leucas*): they belong to the same family, the *Monodontidi*, and there are two belugas for every five narwhals. The total number of narwhals estimated to be in the entire Arctic between Canada, Greenland and Russia is about 80,000.

In winter, when the sea ices over, they feed on fauna from the depths. For the rest of the year, they target particularly Greenland halibut, but also polar cod, shrimps, and squid; however, they fear orcas and walruses, and above all the terrifying polar bear.

WALKING ON THE BUBBLES OF ABRAHAM LAKE

A SURREAL SPECTACLE CREATED BY METHANE IN A FROZEN
LAKE, AT THE FOOT OF THE CANADIAN ROCKY MOUNTAINS,
IN THE PROVINCE OF ALBERTA. SINUOUS SHAPES THAT
YOU CAN ADMIRE BELOW THE CRYSTALLINE SURFACE.

Thousands of crystallized bubbles ripple upward, trapped under the layer of ice. Once they come into contact with the surface water, they flatten out and form sinuous natural sculptures, three-dimensional forms positioned vertically which, through the transparent surface of the lake, seem to plunge into its dark depths. It is a natural phenomenon that creates a spectacle that is both surreal and thrilling; every year, it attracts crowds of tourists and photographers

158 e 159   The extraordinary compositions generated by the methane bubbles trapped under the transparent ice layer of Lake Abraham, an artificial lake along the North Saskatchewan River. When the ice melts in spring, the gas imprisoned is freed into the atmosphere: for this reason, some scientists maintain that the phenomenon contributes to global warming.

WHEN TO GO In winter, from mid-December to the beginning of February, when the layer of ice on the surface of the lake is thicker. The bubbles are visible until March, but the ice becomes less clear and more fragile, and snow may cover some areas.

HOW TO GET THERE Lake Abraham is located 210 miles northwest of Calgary, the capital of Alberta; there is no public transportation to the lake, so the only solution is to rent a car, preferably a 4X4. The area is rather remote and without services during the winter; weather conditions must be constantly watched.

WHAT YOU NEED Clothing for the high mountains: a windproof jacket for polar temperatures, gloves, cap, and thermal underwear, winter hiking boots with anti-slip crampons, sunglasses.

DIFFICULTIES If you are not familiar with activities on the ice, you are advised to go with a knowledgeable person or a local guide.

WEB SITES
www.destinationcanada.com
www.travelalberta.com/ca/articles/finding-serenity-at-abraham-lake-837
www.fototripper.com/abraham-lake-photography-tips

160-161 The red light of the sunset enhances the atmosphere of the place by creating a fairytale scene. Mysterious sounds from the depths of the lake echo on the surface.

who attempt to immortalize it until the ice melts. (Unproven) scientific hypotheses affirm that it is the methane produced that forms the bubbles – as a result of the decomposition of the organic matter of plants, fish and animal carcasses lying on the bottom of the lake.

This very rare phenomenon is repeated every year in Lake Abraham, an artificial lake created in 1972 by the construction of the Bighorn Dam (300 feet high) on the North Saskatchewan River, in the western province of Alberta in Canada. The area of the late is about 20 square miles, and it takes its name from Silas Abraham, one of the first pioneers, who lived in this wild valley at the foot of the Rocky Mountains in the 19th century.

The phenomenon and its visibility have a number of contributory causes.

The very cold climate of the Canadian Rockies – with icy polar winds and winter temperatures around -22 °F – prevents snowfall in an area known for its lack of rain. The layer of ice sealing the lake, at least 4 inches thick, allows the human eye and the camera to explore the depths of its clear cold waters.

The surface is often broken by a network of long cracks, which enable you see the thickness of the ice and the disturbing darkness of the water, and even to hear the seething in its viscera. It is possible to walk on the surface of the lake, but very carefully, avoiding, at all costs the area between the dam and Windy Point; the areas where it is difficult to climb up; those where

rivers and streams flow into the lake; and those covered by snow, which often hide more fragile ice. In any case, it is better not to go too far from the shore.

The spectacle becomes breathtaking when in winter the methane bubbles combine with the green ethereal trails of the Aurora Borealis in the Albertan skies.

USA

STROLLING AMONG CYPRESSES IN THE SWAMP

A NATURAL SANCTUARY WITH TREES WORTHY
OF THE GUINNESS BOOK OF RECORDS:
THE CONGAREE NATIONAL PARK IS THE LARGEST
VIRGIN FLOODPLAIN FOREST IN AMERICA.

The Congaree National Park, which today is a nature reserve, occupies the 34 square miles in the heart of floodplain crossed by the river of the same name. It is home to the largest temperate deciduous forest in the country, which have practically disappeared elsewhere.

The flora is amazing: the average height of the tree canopies is at least 100 feet – but the loblolly pine (*Pinus taeda*) towers up to 160 feet (more or less the equivalent

162-163 Luxuriant inflorescences and aquatic plants with, in the background, a forest of swamp cypresses, conifers native to the southeastern United States.

163 Because of its proximity to the Congaree River, every year there are about a dozen great floods in the park.

ADVICE FOR TRAVELERS

WHEN TO GO The park is open all through the year, but spring (March-June) and autumn (September-December) are the most beautiful seasons with the most varied shades.

HOW TO GET THERE The nearest city is Columbia (30 minutes by car along Bluff Road): it has an airport linking it to the main US cities. You park your car outside the park and reach the entrance on foot. All the paths through the park start from the Harry Hampton Visitor Center.

WHAT YOU NEED Hiking equipment, binoculars for bird-watching, insect repellent spray and enough reserves of food and water; also, camping equipment because the park has no facilities of any kind. For canoe trips it is better to have a map and a compass.

DIFFICULTIES For everyone: the activities take place on foot, on level ground or in a canoe. Those with special needs can use a two-mile gangway.

WEB SITES www.nps.gov/cong/index.htm
www.facebook.com/CongareeNP
www.gousa.in

of a 16-story building), with a circumference of 15 feet. There are oaks, bald cypresses, tupelo trees and many other species, because the Congaree National Park is a hybrid environment. While conifers dominate the forest, on the green plains they give way to high dense vegetation and cypresses. The river is fed by numerous creeks, which more than once give rise to small and enchanting lakes. When the watercourses overflow owing to the heavy seasonal rains, they increase the luxuriance of the forest, a remnant of nature that has not been sacrificed to the needs of humans. However, traces remain: continuing into the park, you are likely to come across embankments, artificial heaps of earth

around 10 feet above the swampy terrain, created by cattle raisers to save their livestock during floods. The park has always been inhabited by squirrels and large mammals like deer, boars, otters and coyotes. Lakes and watercourses teem with fish, but it is also easy to spot turtles and crocodiles. There are endless bird species that have decided to take up residence here, making it a paradise for birdwatchers.

All of the forests are alive, but this one, bathed in the water, seems even more so. There are continuous movements, noises, calls, *chiaroscuri* (above all when the sun's rays filter here and there through the highest fronds), perhaps because of the undergrowth, which is lacking or very thin and does not help the animals to hide.

The paths that extend into the park enable you to cover as many as 26 miles, of which almost four are on the Boardwalk Loop Trail, a wooden gangway suspended over the water. It is the best way to remember to stay clear of rocks and trunks, which are potential hiding places for snakes, spiders and other dangerous animals. The alternative to the paths is the canoe or the kayak, in which you can cross swamps and lakes. If you want to overdo it, you can even reach the park by canoe, following the 50 miles of the Congaree River Blue Trail beginning from Columbia. The Cedar Creek Canoe Trail is the simplest water route, 15 miles with directions to point the way.

The important thing is always to remember to respect the environment: It would be a real crime to ruin this natural sanctuary where visitors can even volunteer for the bird count (a census in the Christmas period, which assesses the health of the avian population of the park). It is one of the many activities than can be practiced with the rangers, your backpack full of wonder and adventure.

164 The quiet waters of the river enable you to travel comfortably by kayak or canoe. While you do this, you may spot a bowfin with its spotted scales or a catfish.

165 One of the most remote corners of the Congaree National Park. Every year, more than 150,000 visitors go deep into the park in search of the most complete silence. The reserve, considered to be a virgin but growing forest, has record-breaking trees, including an American elm 134 feet high and a cherry bark oak 155 feet high.

USA

THE LITTLE FIRE-RED CANYON IN ARIZONA

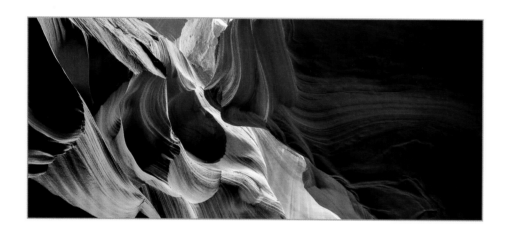

ANTELOPE CANYON, THE SPECTACULAR
FISSURE IN THE AMERICAN SOUTH WEST,
WITH ROCKS THAT CHANGE COLOR
AS FAST AS THE HANDS OF A CLOCK.

The easy hike into the "great wow" begins with some paperwork. Antelope Canyon –
divided into Upper and Lower, a few miles apart – cannot be visited without a guide.
Because of the fragility of the ecosystem, and because water and wind have sculpted
the Navajo territory, it is necessary to book an excursion at an authorized local agency.
If possible, you should do so some months ahead, since there are many people

166 Over the centuries, water has formed the walls of the canyon, creating rocks with evocative profiles,
like this one nicknamed "the Lion King." If you look closely, you can see the face of the king of the forest.

166-167 If you look upward, the shades of color of the Upper Antelope Canyon multiply in contrast to the
blue of the sky.

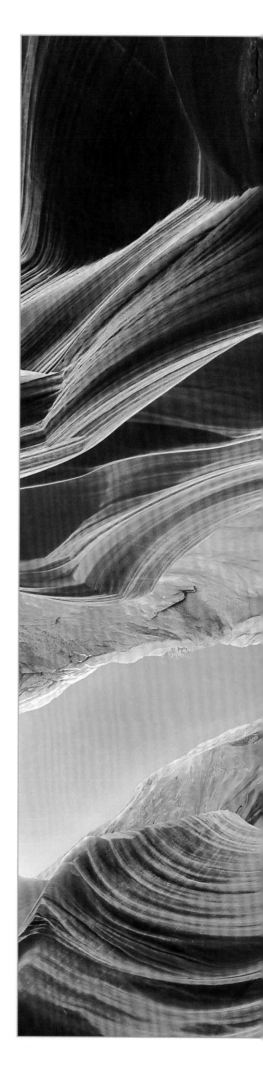

168 Light penetrating from above creates luminous bands that change in intensity at various hours of the day.
169 A tourist at the center of the slit that at some points reaches 121 feet in height.

 ADVICE FOR TRAVELERS

WHEN TO GO The best light conditions are from April to September, but the canyon can be visited throughout the year (in case of rain, meaning flooding risks, the excursion is canceled). The magical hour is midday, when the light penetrates from above and creates the "nebulized" effect for which the canyon is famous.

HOW TO GET THERE It takes 15 minutes from Page to the Navajo Tribal Park on the AZ-98 and the Indian Route 222. Along the way, you see various Navajo agencies for the excursion to the slot canyon (the narrowest part), while the agencies in Page will arrange the transfer to the site access.

WHAT YOU NEED The Lower Canyon requires sneakers or hiking shoes. For the Upper, which is broader and easier to pass through, there is nothing particular to bring, only drinking water and a hat or a bandana to shield yourself from the sand when the wind blows. Backpacks and large bags cannot be carried inside the area.

DIFFICULTIES It is not suitable for claustrophobia sufferers.

WEB SITES
navajonationparks.org
lowerantelope.com
antelopelowercanyon.com
navajotours.com

seeking to hike the technicolor fissure near Page and Lake Powell. Once you've entered it, you'll forget all these tasks in a moment, when the magic of light playing hide-and-seek in the geological monument paints the walls with shades of ochre, red, orange, and dark purple, creating a highly evocative symphony of shadows and textures. This scenario changes its semblance at every step; exactly at midday, "zero hour," the sun's rays penetrate the fissure perpendicularly, and everyone stops, waiting for the miracle: if wisps of sand take flight, the light reflected becomes dense, tactile, almost solid.

The Navajo called the Upper Canyon *Tse bighanilini* ("the place where water flows through the rock"), and the Lower *Hasdestwazi* ("arches of spiral rock"). They went there to enter into spiritual contact with nature: those who choose to visit it in the less crowded months can try to follow their example.

USA

WINTER IN THE GRAND CANYON

MANTLED IN SNOW, THE APPEARANCE OF THE VOLCANIC PEAKS AND ROCKY CLEFTS IS UNEXPECTED, AND IT MAKES HUMANS FEEL MINISCULE.

Imagine you are landing on Mars. When you open the spaceship hatch, you expect to set foot on bare red soil, but you are deep in a blanket of snow, and snowflakes are continuing to fall delicately on rocks and desert plateaus. In this case, however, the doors that open belong to a rail car drawn by a steam locomotive of the Grand Canyon Railway. You only need a few moments to understand that all around you the red has not disappeared. It survives in the vertical walls, where the wind lashes the rock and erodes it, completing the work begun in far-off times by the Colorado River. Under the thinnest veils of white, stone strata appear that recount two billion years of

170-171 The North Rim of the Grand Canyon taken from Yaki Point. It is neither the deepest nor the largest, but this Arizona canyon very spectacularly combines the two characteristics.

171 The Bright Angel Trail, an old Indian trail, is one of the best-known hiking routes in the Grand Canyon.

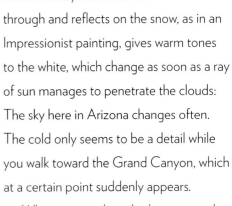

Earth's history. And that red which filters through and reflects on the snow, as in an Impressionist painting, gives warm tones to the white, which change as soon as a ray of sun manages to penetrate the clouds: The sky here in Arizona changes often. The cold only seems to be a detail while you walk toward the Grand Canyon, which at a certain point suddenly appears.

When it snows heavily, the canyon, the chasm, like a gigantic wound 6,000 feet deep, is enhanced with new forms, new pinnacles, new crests, new lines. So you continue to walk through the snow, to get a better view. In the meantime, the sky clears and the clouds, pushed into the background while the sun sets, are ablaze with orange. As the Grand Canyon continues toward infinity, for almost 280 miles, it seems to breathe in and out, it narrows to a few hundred yards and then widens out again, until its walls are almost 19 miles apart.

This is not a film set: it is all real, and the only final curtain is the night. Before nightfall, you need to take shelter because the temperatures are not to be taken lightly. To traverse the more than 50 miles of snow-covered roads along the South Bass Trail (the North Rim is closed in winter), or the narrow icy passages of Boucher Creek, you need crampons and snowshoes. But be aware that the paths to descend into the canyon are rather demanding, and that the ice greatly worsens the situation.

ADVICE FOR TRAVELERS

WHEN TO GO The area of the South Rim, served by the railroad, is open yearlong, but it is wise to book many months in advance.

HOW TO GET THERE You leave on the Grand Canyon Railway from the town of Williams. You can reach it by the mythical Route 66. Usually there is one departure per day from Williams and one from the Grand Canyon, but in high season a second daily train is scheduled.

WHAT YOU NEED Winter hiking equipment and a well-supplied backpack, including changes of dry clothing, snowshoes and crampons.

DIFFICULTIES The train journey is for everyone, but the excursions on the snow must definitely be taken seriously, above all because of the ice; it is advisable to hire a local guide. From November to February, the weather conditions are variable, with alternating sun, rain, and snow, and temperature ranges as wide as 30 degrees, depending on the altitude.

WEB SITES www.nps.gov/grca/index.htm, www.thetrain.com, www.grandcanyoncvb.org, www.grandcanyonlodges.com

172 A section of the Bright Angel Trail after a snowstorm, a situation that has always attracted particularly intrepid hikers.

173 The wapiti (elk), a subspecies of the red deer, reaches a considerable size: males can weigh up to 1,300 pounds.

THE HAVASU FALLS: A WORLD IN MINIATURE

A NATURAL AMPHITHEATER DUG INTO CLIFFS OF RED ROCK TYPICAL
OF THE GREAT CANYONS OF THE AMERICAN WEST, ITS BEAUTY ENHANCED
BY WATERFALLS AND NATURAL POOLS OF TURQUOISE WATER.

The Havasupai, a tribe of the native people, have always lived in what for many of us is the perfect representation of earthly paradise: the valley of the Havasu Falls. Emerald-colored water, blood-colored rocks, the green of bushes and the white of travertine concretions: probably not even Adam and Eve had a similar Eden to live in. It is small but extremely varied. Owing to the water's high mineral content, which produces

frequent subsidence and modifications in the riverbed, waterfalls continue to change continuously because, even in limited time periods, the course of the river is slightly modified.

Credit for this miracle of nature goes to the Havasu Creek, a tributary of the Colorado River, with which it contributes to creating the spectacular natural scenery of the Grand Canyon. But the Havasu Falls are outside the jurisdiction of

the Grand Canyon National Park, in the territory controlled by the eponymous Indian tribe. For this reason, they are not assaulted by the hordes of tourists which every day crowd these areas.

174 The intense colors of the landscape around Havasu Falls; there are four other waterfalls in the reserve. They can easily be reached on foot.

175 The terraced pools of travertine fed by the waterfall. The limestone is very resistant to atmospheric agents and erosion.

WHEN TO GO The site is closed in December and January. The best period is from March to May and from September to October. There is torrid heat from June to August, and the driest period for the natural pools is October. Always check for temporary closures caused by unexpected downpours, which are also possible during visits. You should book well in advance, even over a year before.

HOW TO GET THERE Peach Springs and Seligman are the nearest localities; you can drive as far as the Hualapai Hilltop, about 9 miles from the falls: it is essentially a large parking lot. From the Hualapai Hilltop you continue on foot, on mule back or in a helicopter (this is not bookable; you need to stand in line in the parking lot and hope to board one). No day excursions are permitted.

WHAT YOU NEED Hiking equipment and reserves of food and water: there are no facilities until you reach Supai (thirty minutes' walk from the falls).

DIFFICULTIES Reaching it on foot is demanding and rather time-consuming. Calculate three days for the visit: one for descending, one for enjoying the falls, one for ascending.

WEB SITES
www.nps.gov/grca/planyourvisit/havasupai.htm
theofficialhavasupaitribe.com
www.havasupaireservations.com
www.westernriver.com
fsguides.com/destinations/havasu-falls-grand-canyon/

176 The high concentration of calcium carbonate increases the blue coloring of the water and makes it appear more dense and fluid. Great floods continuously modify the height of the waterfall and the course of the river.

177 There are many sporting opportunities along the 10 miles of the Havasu Creek, from rafting to river boarding to swimming in safety.

Thus not all travelers will be able to boast of an experience of this kind. The Havasupai (in the Yumana language of the plateaus it means "the people of the green-blue waters") continue to be strongly attached to their land, and in order to defend it they have drawn up regulations that prevent very short vacations. In practice, you must earn entry into the terrestrial paradise. Visitors must obtain a booking allowing them to stay in the area, in a campsite or in the lodge located in the town of Supai. The excursion itself requires more than four hours' hiking, at the end of which you really enter what at first sight seems to be a mirage. The dusty road increases your anticipation, but then the impact is astonishing: the 100-foot drop of the Havasu Falls, the 200-foot drop of the Mooney Falls, the blindingly saturated colors, the invigorating blue on the edge of the falls. You really need three days,

or more, to see it. You can arrive from Hualapai Hilltop more easily and in less time by helicopter or, as a compromise solution, on mule back.

For the adventurous, the alternative is to arrive from the Colorado River, rafting up the river through the Grand Canyon for a week. It is an extreme experience, almost like that of the early explorers who, with few means of transport and little baggage, were willing to face the risks of a very wild nature.

You camp in deserted clearings, by the light of the moon, and you cover 190 miles from Lee's Ferry, in the vicinity of the Utah border, as far as the mouth of the Havasu Creek. Alternatively, you can follow the shorter itineraries, a combination of hiking and more cautious kayak stages on the river. One thing is certain: bathing in the crystalline waters is worth all the effort (and adds to the array of great travel memories).

USA

THE CANYON OF THE TREES IN BLOOM

RIVERS HAVE DUG ENORMOUS CANYONS IN THE SOUTHERN ROCKY MOUNTAINS. CANYON DE CHELLY IS NEITHER THE BEST KNOWN, NOR THE LARGEST, BUT IT IS CERTAINLY ONE OF THE MOST FASCINATING.

You set out walking, behind the Navajo scout, who has a colored headband for his hair. You stop when the scout decides it is worth it, and he explains or relates. The sound of hooves on the rocks or muffled by dust and the rhythmic rocking of the horses' gait help you to enter another dimension.

Canyon de Chelly is a complex geographical creation following the course of Chinle Wash and that of a hundred other creeks dug into the red rock walls up to 980 feet high. Still today, on the floor of the canyon there are fruit trees, vegetable gardens and vegetation: it is enchanting in the endless barren sea of these mountains. Once you

178   A group of tourists rides across the Canyon de Chelly, whose name means "stone canyon."

178-179   Spider Rock is one of the symbols of the canyon, but above all for the Navajos it is the home of Na'ashjé'íí Asdzáá, the "Spider Woman," the goddess of creation and protection.

have descended to the bottom the scene is colored completely with reds and blues through your sunglasses (be sure to wear them), saturated and dense colors like the rocks and skies of Arizona. They are flecked with the silvery points of peach and cherry leaves, which are breathtakingly beautiful especially when the trees blossom. Humans have lived here for thousands of years. There are many stories and legends, and the guides are generous in relating stories and giving answers.

A visit to the White House is a must, which is the main (but not the only) settlement of the Anasazi (the ancient native people) in the canyon. Incidentally, this is the only point you are allowed to reach free and without a guide (White House Ruins Trail: about 45 minutes to descend and then re-ascend, depending on your level of fitness) as far as the wire fence that protects it.

The obelisk-shaped stone, Spider Rock (830 feet high), is much photographed. Also in the middle of the canyon, there is an enormous rock called Navajo Fortress, which was the Navajos' last refuge when confronted by the Spanish army. It is related that many threw themselves off when it was clear that they had no chance of escaping their fate, which awaited them also in the grotto called Massacre Cave, which is also open to visitors. But there are other things to do: the rims, northern and southern; that is, the paved roads that follow the contours of the canyon, with many detours toward the edge. They should be considered an integral, essential part of the visit. Signs all along the way indicate the points of interest and detours toward the lookouts on the edge of the canyon, where maps and descriptions describe the sites in detail. All combined, however, they still fall short of explaining how Canyon de Chelly creates such enchantment.

WILD NATURE
IN BLACK AND WHITE

Canyon de Chelly has been inhabited for 5,000 years by communities of hunters/ gatherers, basket-makers, Anasazi, Hopi and finally the Navajos. First the Spaniards and then the Union Cavalry, led by the famous Kit Karson, sought to annihilate them. But the Navajos are still there, and in the thirties the canyon received eminent visitors, above all great photographers. Among them was the indefatigable Ansel Adams, who for many years covered the national parks of the Rocky Mountains in search of the American wilderness, in a van perfectly equipped for developing and printing films. He worked above all on exposure, lighting and resolution, and his black and white photos of Canyon de Chelly are now symbols indivisible from the place itself, like other extraordinary spaces in the mountains.

 ADVICE FOR TRAVELERS

WHEN TO GO Practically at any time. In winter, the landscape changes completely with the snow, but it is just as fascinating.

HOW TO GET THERE Canyon de Chelly is the heart of the Navajo reserve, located 186 miles from Flagstaff. Wherever you are, the Visitor Center of the Canyon de Chelly National Monument can easily be reached, with a detour of three miles on 191 North, the south-north highway. The visit (for which there is a payment) requires a Navajo guide. It is on foot (but the canyon is immense), by car or, as we have seen, on horseback.

WHAT YOU NEED It depends on the season, but you need mountain clothing. It is comparatively hot in the daytime, but you are moving between 8,200 and 11,400 feet above sea level. You should take a windproof jacket, high hiking shoes, hat, sun protection cream, and sunglasses.

DIFFICULTIES As navigators and cell phones do not work within the reserve, it is very important to pay the greatest attention to road signs and the numerous notices along the roads.

WEB SITES
www.nps.gov/cach/index.htm
www.go-arizona.com
www.nationalparks.org
www.visittheusa.com

180 An unusually wide section of the canyon where we can clearly see a bend in the Chinle Wash, the watercourse that dug it.

181 top Graffiti by Spanish knights on the walls of the arm called the Canyon del Muerto.

181 bottom The ruins of the little Pueblo village of Mummy Cave where two mummies were discovered in 1882.

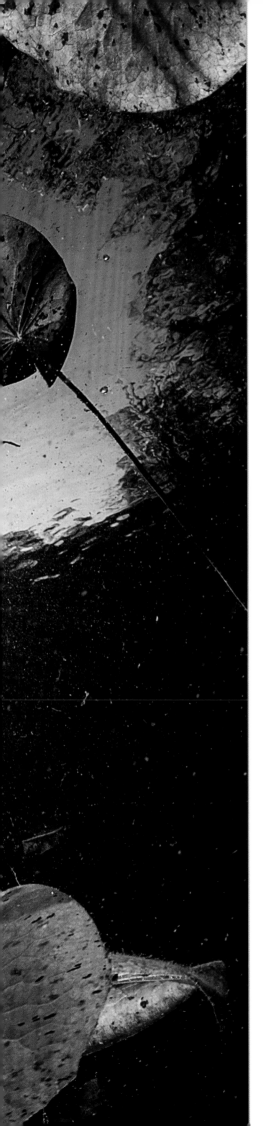

MEXICO

DIVING INTO HISTORY

MYSTERY, NATURE, AND WONDER. A PARALLEL
MICROCOSM IS UNVEILED TO THE DIVER,
WHO FEELS THE THRILL OF DIVING AND VENTURING
INTO THE DEPTHS OF A CENOTE IN YUCATÁN.

The surface of the water is only a few inches from the level of the bank. You can sit there with your feet dangling or slide gently into the water. It is easy to get into the cenote Aktun Ha. There are no ladders to climb down (apart from in the driest season), nor dives as in other cases. The cenote Aktun Ha is located a few steps from the Tulum-Cobá road.

The water is crystalline and so calm that it seems a crime against nature to disturb it when you swim, but there is much more you can do.

182-183 Brightly-colored underwater water lilies in the transparent water of the cenote Aktun Ha, not far from Tulum: the most famous cenotes are found along the Riviera Maya.

183 Aerial view of a cenote completely covered by the forest in the State of Quintana Roo, on the western side of the peninsula.

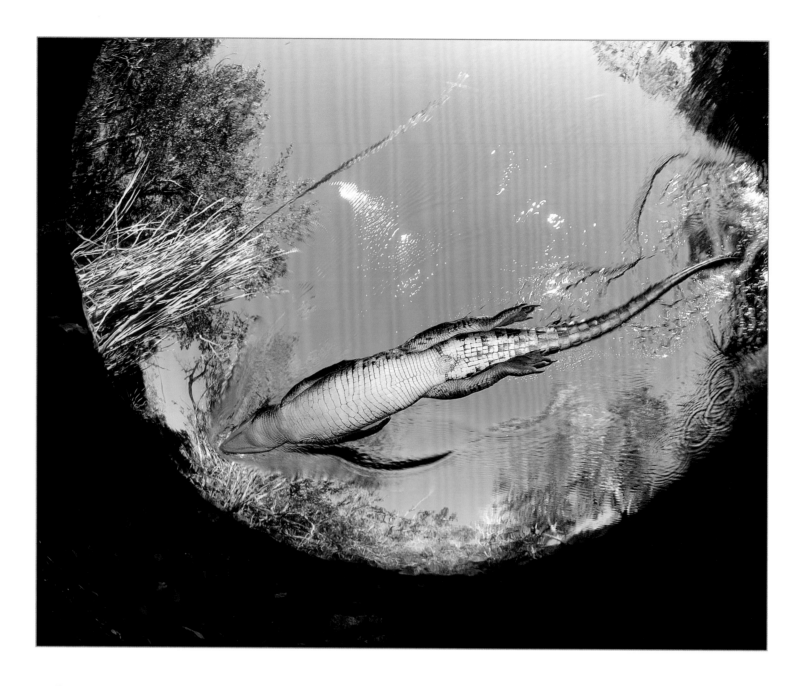

First, let's take a step back: the
cenotes are large (sometimes very
large) fresh water pools. The ones we
see on the surface, among the trees
of the forest, are like this because of
the collapse of the roof of the cave
containing them. In fact, many are still
subterranean and are mostly accessible.

A cenote is not only a marvelous
natural swimming pool, but also part
of an intricate network of caves and
subterranean rivers, linked to the sea.
Protected by the Mexican jungle,
among white sandy beaches and
unexpected waterfalls, these Kars

phenomena sometimes also hide salt
water and marine fauna. The Yucatán is
the kingdom of the cenotes, which were
venerated by the Maya as a precious
water reserve and a route to the
Inframundo, the afterlife.

The great pools, blue chasms, were
considered to be important channels of
communication with the gods, so much
so that in many cenotes they have found
votive objects and the remains
of human sacrifices. For example, Aktun
Ha is a complex cenote composed of
an open part and a larger underground
part, which is linked to the former by

two apertures, both viable for divers.
This means that, besides swimming,
you can do snorkeling in the part facing
the forest, a few feet deep and dense
with great pink, yellow and lilac lilies.
An unbelievable pool, which on some
days combines with jets of tannic acid
from the underground river: they
transform it to create reflections
reminiscent of a sunset. When you
swim below the surface, the effect
is extraordinary.

For the more experienced divers,
there is the covered part where a
slow underground river flows, dispersing

WHEN TO GO Yucatan's high temperatures make it possible to visit all through the year; the high season, with a milder climate, runs from December to April, and the more humid season, with the risk of rain, from June to October.

HOW TO GET THERE Merida and Cancun are the main international airports in the area; to travel in the interior, you can use coach lines that reach the tourist locations or rent a car for greater independence.

WHAT YOU NEED For diving, which is more demanding, you must provide certification. For underwater speleology, with more difficult movement through tunnels, you need a license. In any case, all equipment and a wetsuit can be rented *in loco*.

DIFFICULTIES Ropes have been placed at the extremities for the less experienced to provide support and safety, and in the larger and better-known cenotes safety people are always present. When you dive, always follow the guides and the marked routes.

WEB SITES
www.visitmexico.com
cenotesmexico.org
www.divecenotesmexico.com
bluelife.com

into the limestone. It is partly illuminated by the sun through an opening in the vault, and partly pitch black: even if it is not particularly dangerous, it is not to be treated lightly. Maximum depth: about 65 feet. Obviously, a guide is compulsory.

Anyone who enters the water, from swimmers to divers, can have exceptional encounters. Small turtles, small crocodiles, various fish, especially those that the Mexicans call "tetras," the little shiny fish that you often see in aquariums and that particularly enjoy playing with the divers' bubbles.

There are at least 7,000 cenotes in the Yucatán. Erosion has affected the stone to the point that the roof of the great caves has been brought down, creating pools of varying circumferences. This is also because the porous limestone terrain of the area means there is little surface water in the peninsula: it collects underground, creating a fascinating subterranean world studded with stalactites and stalagmites. In Maya, the term means "water cavity" but also "sacred pool": among the many legends surrounding the cenotes, there is also the one of

184 The Mexican crocodile is one of the inhabitants of these waters. Although it is comparatively small – an adult male reaches 10 feet – it can be dangerous for humans.

185 top The multicolored aquatic fauna in the cenotes makes them ideal for snorkeling.

185 bottom The Mesoamerican turtle (*Trachemys*) inhabits these natural pools in the Mexican jungle.

186 The cenotes have always played a fundamental role in Mayan civilization: besides their being an inexhaustible source of freshwater, the indigenous people believed that these natural grottoes possessed healing powers.

187 A diver exploring inside a cenote: the largest cavities extend in labyrinthine routes that it is indispensable to know before venturing into them.

miraculous cures through the gods.

No one can resist bathing in these waters. As at Aktun Ha, generally you can do snorkeling, but if you want to concentrate on diving, guides must be present and you must follow the rules. The unexplored tunnels and the vastness of the rocky labyrinths could represent a potential danger for the inexperienced and make it difficult to get back.

The cenotes are not all the same: there are different types. There are completely open ones, where the vegetation creates a postcard scene, and closed ones, which can be reached through gaps made in the rock, like the two cenotes of Dnitzup. In this case, the setting is darker and more mysterious and the effect of water with many shades of blue is unique. These are the Samulá and X'Kekén cenotes, very close to each other and a short distance from Valladolid, located inland. The impressive waterfall, completely surrounded by roots, makes the X'Kekén cenote one of the most photographed in the Yucatán. Most organized cenotes (with changing rooms, guides, etc.) are found in eastern Yucatán, between Valladolid and Tulum.

YUCATÁN, EARTH AND WATER

The rocks of the Yucatán are 200 million years old, and are made of light, porous, friable limestone. Moreover, the Yucatán is a tableland a few feet above sea level, and almost completely flat. As a result, the rains penetrate everywhere; they crumble, cut, and open channels as far as the subterranean clay, so that underneath the ground in Yucatàn there is a network of interconnected watercourses, pools, lakes, grottoes, caves, and tunnels that are also linked to the sea. On the surface, it is the classic Kars landscape where the local sink-holes are called "cenotes," from the Maya dzanot, *which not very imaginatively translates as "water cavity." They are bodies of water of varying size and depth. And they are environments with an extremely fragile ecology: if you want to bathe, you are recommended to avoid sun protection creams or other substances that can damage the ecological balance.*

MEXICO

THE BUTTERFLIES THAT COLOR THE WOODS OF THE SIERRA

MILLIONS OF BUTTERFLIES FLUTTER ON THEIR DELICATE WINGS – WHITE, ORANGE, AND BLACK – TO GO FROM CANADA TO MICHOACÁN IN MEXICO, WHERE THEY SPEND THE WINTER. AND THEN THEY RETURN TO CANADA, TO AVOID THE TORRID TROPICAL SUMMER.

Every year, millions of monarch butterflies cover 3-4,000 miles from the Rocky Mountains of Canada and the United States as far as the central Mexican Cordillera to fulfill their reproductive and evolutionary cycle.

From December to February, they cover pines, firs, and cedars in Mexico and fill the air with shades of orange and wing beats. It is a fantastic spectacle in the landscape of mountain woods, great trees,

cliffs, paths, and valleys on the Sierra de Anáhuac, the transverse chain of volcanoes separating Toluca from Morelia. The butterflies concentrate on the flowers they feed on (their favorites are called *asclepiadaceae*). Then suddenly, there is a noise or a gust of wind that causes them to take flight, all together. The sky changes color, everything moves, the sounds are breaths, quivers, vibrations. In Michoacán there are five monarch

sanctuaries, all on the Sierra separating Toluca from Morelia (northeast of the capital): Piedra Herrada, La Mesa, El Capulín, Sierra Chincua, and El Rosario.

188 Hundreds of monarch butterflies cover the bark of a pine, where they spend the winter in semi-hibernation.

189 The life-cycle of these insects is fascinating and mysterious: only those born at the end of summer are equipped to face the long flight.

 ## ADVICE FOR TRAVELERS

WHEN TO GO Usually the monarchs begin to arrive in Mexico at the beginning of November and continue their tropical season until March.

HOW TO GET THERE By coach: 5-6 hours from Morelia, 7 hours from Mexico City, but there are no direct coaches. Day excursions are impracticable. Keeping in mind the present Mexican situation and the fact that Michoacán is one of the states involved in drug trafficking, today you are strongly advised to go on this excursion with an organization and a guide from Mexico City. This is also because it is not easy to find accommodation locally during high season.

WHAT YOU NEED Mountain clothing. In the daytime it is comparatively hot, but you are walking at an altitude of between 8,200 and 11,400 feet. High hiking shoes, hat, sunblock cream, sunglasses and equipment also for the cold.

DIFFICULTIES Good physical condition is recommended.

WEB SITES hablemosdeinsectos.com/santuario-de-la-mariposa-monarca
www.mexicodesconocido.com.mx/mariposa-monarca-santuarios-mexico.html
www.monarch-butterfly.com

190 The monarch is the only insect species in the world that migrates so far, similarly to birds.

191 top Even though none of them faces the flight twice, the butterflies know the route by instinct.

191 bottom The Monarch Butterfly Biosphere Reserve has been recognized as a World Heritage Site since 2008.

The first is the highest, on the slopes of the Nevado de Toluca (15,350 feet), the third is perhaps best equipped, and the last is historical, the official address of the Reserva de la biosfera de la Mariposa Monarca (about 80 miles from the capital). There are no direct coaches for these places, so it is necessary to change at least once. Then there are from 1 to 2 miles to cover on foot or on horseback to get into the woods. In the end, you only need to wait and *they* will organize the most choreographic of shows. Even though reaching it is difficult, the "monarch world" is an unforgettable place.

A FASCINATING MIGRATION

There are many amazing aspects of this extraordinary natural phenomenon, but there is one in particular that is really difficult to comprehend. The life of the monarch (danaus plexippus) *lasts only for weeks. This means for example that the butterflies that leave from the north are not the same as those that left from the south in the previous season. And to make everything still more miraculous, many of the butterflies that leave from the north nonetheless live for up to eight months, thanks to a complex biological mechanism indispensable for reproduction. In any case, there are different generations involved. And yet the monarchs have come and gone for millennia and often lay their eggs on the same trees as their ancestors. These are marvels of nature. After all, even the word* mariposa *("butterfly" in Spanish) has a magical ring.*

COLOMBIA

THE LIQUID RAINBOW

MANY INTENSE SHADES MAKE THIS RIVER, OF CRYSTAL CLEAR WATER
AND A ROCKY BED, A UNIQUE COLOR-SPECTACLE IN THE WORLD,
LASTING ONLY A FEW MONTHS IN THE YEAR BUT FOREVER ENCHANTING.

The Serranía de La Macarena Colombian national park, south of the capital, Bogotá, reveals itself as a jewel with unexpected grandeur to visitors. It is the Caño Cristales, called the liquid rainbow: the river seems to have stolen its colors directly from fairytales, and mixed them together, to make an exceptionally visionary picture.

The riverbed is covered with moss and algae: when the water level is lower, in the transition period between the rainy and dry seasons, the sun's rays enable the

vegetation to regenerate and change color; and the river changes along with it. The main ingredient of this magic potion is *macarenia clavigera*, a particular freshwater plant, with velvety inflorescences and rich in carotenoids.

The psychedelic spectacle begins with an explosion of colors. Green is joined by red, yellow, orange and fuchsia, blue, white and black. As the weeks pass, new hues are added to the dark shades of the rocks. The river flows in rapids and waterfalls, between natural pools.

Above all, in the part called "los ochos," it flows into cavities sunk into the earth, almost as though they were buckets of paint in which the river dips its brushes.

The game of colored reflections can be seen for at least 60 miles, reflected on the beauty of the surrounding landscape, interspersed with plains and steep slopes.

192 On sunny days, the colors of the river light up and enable you to see the spectacle of the "river of five colors."

193 The phenomenon only lasts a few weeks each year, between September and November.

WHEN TO GO The park is open from mid-June to the end of November, but the best period to see the phenomenon is in the last two months, starting from September.

HOW TO GET THERE You leave from La Macarena, which can be reached by light aircraft from Bogotá; from the port, you can follow the Rio Guayabero in a launch, or else reach the entrance to the park in a 4x4. The local agencies organize guided excursions toward the river, on foot or on horseback. The routes can change depending on the climatic conditions and the number of visitors.

WHAT YOU NEED Light clothing that provides protection from the sun and dries quickly; comfortable, ankle-high waterproof shoes. Be advised: inside the park the use of sun protection creams, mosquito repellents, and other chemical products is prohibited.

DIFFICULTIES Accessible to everyone, but bear in mind that for most of the excursion you are crossing the river, with water up to your ankles or your knees.

WEB SITES
www.canocristales.com
www.cano-cristales.com
thecolombianway.co

In November, the algae dry and enter the reproductive phase, losing their color. The magic temporarily ceases and the Caño Cristales is once again a "normal" river in the green province of Meta.

While for a long time the park was inaccessible to the public because it was on the route of the Colombian revolutionary forces, today it can be visited, thanks to a peace agreement signed with the government. However, the most serious threat at the moment is climate change.

You cannot enjoy so much beauty without an authorized guide guaranteeing the safety of the route; in fact, the protected area in some places is still very wild and without signs. Apart from being the habitat of pumas, jaguars, and iguanas, a more welcome presence, the hoatzin (*Opisthocomus hoazin*) might peep out: It has a rock singer's fringe and multicolor plumage. But there are no fish: the river has no sediment and provides no food for water creatures.

As you walk, you almost want to stop at every step because the river bed, the water, the sky, the vegetation come together in ways that are always unpredictable and fascinating.

194 Little streams spring from the rocks and feed the multicolored river.

195 top In different sections, the colors of the Caño Cristales have shifting green, red, yellow, blue, and white shades.

195 bottom The hike to the river is accompanied by specialist guides; it is quite demanding, but the effort is amply repaid.

BRAZIL

SETTING SAIL FOR AMAZONIA

A TRULY ELABORATE SYSTEM ENABLING HUNDREDS OF THOUSANDS OF ANIMAL AND BOTANICAL SPECIES TO LIVE, THANKS TO ITS FLOW OF BILLIONS OF CUBIC FEET OF WATER. IT IS THE AMAZON RIVER, THE LONGEST RIVER ON EARTH.

Night falls suddenly, toward six in the evening. You are intent on following the Indios in the forest about 18 miles from Manaus – the capital of the Brazilian state of Amazonas, which is five times larger than Italy, but with just 4 million inhabitants. So you do not even notice that the light gradually disappears, giving way to total darkness. While during the day the sounds of the forest do not seem to be too threatening, at night everything seems amplified: whistles, calls, cries, trees shaking because of curious monkeys spying on the little camp, distant noises, and a sort of modulated hissing, the sign that the *onça pintada*, the formidable jaguar, the terror of those living in the forest, is too near. For supper you have some crackers, a small bottle of water and a little

196-197 A stretch of the Amazon River, between the forest trees, photographed from a drone.

197 A riverboat sails along the great river near Iquitos. The Amazon is also a link for transporting goods.

crocodile fallen to the machete of one of the guides, cooked over the fire.

The camp, the result of a sudden, irrational "longing for adventure," is a microscopic point in endless Amazonia, an endless sequence of similar landscapes: *igapós* (flooded forests), fields, trees, more fields, cultivated lands, and water everywhere, as far as the eye can see. The waters are those of the majestic Amazon River which, at 4,345 miles, is the longest river on earth, but also those of its great tributaries (to mention a few, the Rivers

Yavarí, Juruá, Madeira, and Negro, all over 600 miles long); and others, more than a thousand, that are the nervous system of the Amazon basin. It is precisely on the Amazon River, the river that resembles a sea, where often you cannot see the banks, that an extraordinary experience awaits. If you go from Manaus to Belém, the capital of Pará (994 miles over almost 5 days' sailing) on ferries, distant relations of the *gaiolas* (the old, spartan boats that you can still see sailing), but larger, safer and more punctual, it is one of those voyages that will

remain with you forever. You begin immediately near Manaus with the *encontro das águas*, between the River Solimões and the River Negro which, together, create the Amazon: before the two rivers combine, they flow in parallel without contact for about 6 miles because of the different acidity, temperature, and speed of the waters. You will also find this phenomenon during the voyage to Santarém, though it is much less evident. There are other emotions: you spot *botos* (*Inia geoffrensis*), pink river dolphins, with

►► ADVICE FOR TRAVELERS

WHEN TO GO The most highly recommended months are July, August, and September: avoid the periods between December and May, when precipitation is frequent and the climate is hotter and more humid.

HOW TO GET THERE The boats sale from the port of Manaus, which is linked to the main Brazilian airports by several flights a day.

WHAT YOU NEED Comfortable, breathable clothing. Pants with large side pockets that also become Bermuda shorts are ideal, as are T-shirts, a light windbreaker, and a cap with anti-mosquito netting. It is better always to take water and mineral salt supplements.

DIFFICULTIES The experience does not entail difficulties, but rather prudence, good equipment, and the indispensable presence of a guide. In addition, in Amazonia yellow fever vaccination and antimalarial prophylaxis is compulsory.

WEB SITES
portalamazonia.com.br
vivamanaus.com
parintins.com
www.artransporte.com.br

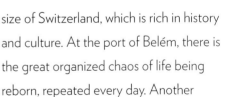

a very long rostrum; the Indios consider them to be animals of divine origin.

At the traditional market *Ver o peso* in Belém you frequently meet the dried sexual organs of these mammals, which are considered to possess aphrodisiac powers. Another surprise is the meetings with the *ribeirinhos*, the inhabitants of the riverbanks, mainly fishermen and very many children, who try to sell everything, from local handicrafts, to medicines from the forest, to freshly caught fish and tasty and nutritious tapioca pancakes cooked on the fire.

The voyage stops at incredible places for beauty and culture, like Parintins, where every year one of the most important folklore festivals in Latin America is celebrated; and Santarém, which can be visited thanks to a ferry maintenance stop; it was founded in 1661, and is one of the oldest cities in the Amazon region, besides being one of the most important trading centers. The last marvel before arriving in Belém is the river delta (150 miles long) with the ilha de Marajó in the middle. It is an island the

size of Switzerland, which is rich in history and culture. At the port of Belém, there is the great organized chaos of life being reborn, repeated every day. Another world, other stories, other horizons.

198 The Amazon Forest extends for almost 2 million square miles, which becomes more than 2 and a half million with the semi-wooded area surrounding it.

199 top A red bald uakari, which can be recognized by its scarlet face.

199 bottom The colored feathers of a scarlet macaw.

200-201 The pink coloring of the boto, the largest of the river dolphins, is typical of adults.

IN DANGER
OF EXTINCTION

They are curious, like their saltwater cousins. They interact with man and have a much longer and pronounced "snout" than dolphins have: They have adapted to hunting for fish, turtles and crustaceans in the midst of the intricate tree root systems.

Present in the Rivers Amazonas, Solimões, and Araguaia, and in the Bolivian sub-basin, this freshwater mammal has become the symbol of Amazonia. The most famous are the boto cor de rosa (Amazon dolphins, Inia geoffrensis), so called because of the pinkish pigmentation of their skin (especially in adult males); but there are also black dolphins, which the Indios call tucuxi and the Brazilians call boto preto (Sotalia fluviatilis). The males can reach 10 feet in length and weigh 407 pounds, and the females 7 feet and 330 pounds.

It is an endangered symbol, however: a study in 2018 published by Plos One, *a scientific journal of the US Public Library of Science, estimated that the population of boto cor de rosa will halve every ten years and that of boto preto every nine. This takes into account that the females only give birth to one calf every 4-5 years, and that these animals are massacred to use their meat as bait in fishing for bagre (a cat fish that is very popular on the market).*

THE NATURAL POOLS OF LENÇÓIS

DESERT AND WATER, A UNIQUE SPACE IN THE WORLD, WHICH HAS BEEN REGENERATING FOR OVER 10,000 YEARS; WHERE NATURE REIGNS UNCHALLENGED AND OBSERVES HUMANKIND, A FLEETING PILGRIM.

The light is strong, crystalline, warm, diffused: it reflects from the sea, through the serpentine intricacy of the mangroves, and illuminates the pristine dunes that form the horizon. You realize that travelers feel they are in a special place when they venture into the far *Nordeste* of Brazil: they are aware of experiencing an extraordinary spectacle. There is a positive tension, that air of expectation which presages something grandiose and unique.

This area of 580 square miles (practically the same area as the city of São Paulo) extends from the sea as far as the desert interior of the state of Maranhão. The dunes interspersed with crystalline natural pools, the shores inhabited by fishing communities, and the two rivers (Preguiças and Alegre) forming the territory as far as the ocean constitute a spectacular

202-203 Every photo taken at the Lençóis Maranhenses National Park is totally unique: the next day, the dunes, moved by the wind, will no longer be exactly the same.

203 The park, founded in 1981, extends for 155,000 hectares, flanked by 43 miles of ocean beaches.

204 Rainwater is trapped by the sand dunes, creating harmonious repeating patterns. They attract around 60,000 visitors a year to this region.

205 Aerial view of the Lençóis Maranhenses National Park. Jeeps are parked at the entrance to the Park: many animals (insects, migratory birds, and tortoises) are hidden among the soft dunes and, for this reason, motor vehicles are not allowed.

scenario even for Brazil, which is already famous for exceptional natural phenomena. Lençóis, the sheets, so called because of the pure white dunes that appear as unmade beds, is a small miracle that has repeated itself regularly for over ten thousand years. It is pure, crystalline freshwater: it appears between January and June with high points until September, and then magically disappears for the rest of the year. For the Brazilians, it is a kind of magical experience as a gift from the earth, which is to be respected. For the scientists who have been studying the phenomenon for years, it is straightforward: Due to the heavy rain (on average, 300 times greater than in the Sahara), the groundwater rises and fills the "hollows" between the dunes, reaching an average depth of 3 feet. In these rainy months, the sand becomes wet and the wind cannot carry it: It creates those natural pools where you can dive and where fish proliferate, a gift for the local people. When the rain ceases, the wind from the sea (gusting at up to 43 mph) begins its work again: it shifts the dunes (which can even move 4 inches a day), creating new shapes that recall Oscar Niemeyer's modernist buildings. It digs into the desert, pushes tons of sand closer to the interior, and devours huts, mangroves and palm trees. There are other points of contact with this nature: sunset bird-watching at Atins near the River Preguiças, to see the arrival of scores of red ibis, which perch on trees for the night; trekking, with various degrees of difficulty, in the heart of the park; and, for sports enthusiasts, kite-surfing to defy the waves along the coast, from August to September; and if you want to take aerial photographs, you can pay 350 reais per person (about 95 dollars), and fly in a Piper over the park to have a complete idea of the majesty of the place.

One rare feature of Lençóis is that you can return there as often as you like because the landscape never appears the same. It is Nature that advances, grows, and changes in a rigid order that only she, the custodian for a thousand years, knows how to manage. Desert and water, light and untamed nature, up there on the border of the Ocean, on the edge of the world.

 ## ADVICE FOR TRAVELERS

WHEN TO GO To find the natural polls, the ideal months are from January to June. In some areas, pools remain until October, the driest period.

HOW TO GET THERE The journey has become relatively fast with the re-surfacing of the road: It is 160 miles from São Luís airport. Tour packages include a 4X4 with a driver and a pousada on the spot. You can hire a car (or better, a jeep) and drive yourself, keeping in mind that within the park, cars must have a permit. You can also reach Lençóis on coaches that depart from the terminal in São Luís twice a day: the journey takes four hours.

WHAT YOU NEED Light clothing, as for the sea, a light jacket for the evening, a hat (indispensable!), flip-flops and tennis shoes, and a good supply of sunblock cream and insect repellent. Hiking shoes for the sports enthusiasts.

DIFFICULTIES There are different trips, from the most to the least strenuous. The less fit can go to the Santo Amaro lagoons: since they are inside the park, you can practically reach the base of the dunes by authorized transport. Or you can stay near Barreirinhas, and there you can book tours of various durations. For those who want something more intense, there is hiking in the heart of the Park, from Atins to Santo Amaro.

WEB SITES www.icmbio.gov.br/parnalencoismaranhenses/guia-do-visitante.html
www.turismo.ma.gov.br
portalbarreirinhas.com.br

GALÁPAGOS, THE ENCHANTED ARCHIPELAGO

THE EXTRAORDINARY WILDLIFE RESERVE AND
THE UNUSUAL AND BIZARRE ANIMALS OF THE
ISLANDS OF CHARLES DARWIN AND EVOLUTION.

Scores of albatrosses scuttle up a slope all in a row. They are disciplined and do not push; they await their turn to take flight from the cliff. They all take off from the same point, as if they recognized this rocky spur as the runway for their endless journeys. By taking advantage of air currents, they can fly for hundreds of miles without touching the ground. Albatrosses (*Diomedea irrorata*) are the largest birds on the

206   A sea lion, a species endemic to these islands, on the immaculate beach of Gardner Bay, on the island of Española. Because they do not fear humans, there can be direct contact in the water.

206-207   The fascinating promontory of the island of Bartolomé seen from a lookout: when the sky is clear, you can make out as many as ten islands.

planet, weighing 28 pounds with an average wingspan of 6.5 feet. Owing to their weight and size, it is very difficult for them to take off from the ground (impossible from the sea), and so they use cliffs as takeoff platforms.

The albatross cliff is reached from the beach at Punta Suarez on the island of Española by walking among the sulas that seem to have just dipped their legs in a pool of red or blue paint. Among these, a family apart is constituted by the Nazca boobies, which have decidedly worrying fratricidal behavior. There are also flocks made up of scores of cuckoos, restless small birds that are not at all frightened by human presence. The tourist-explorer is already won over by this route, which immerses him or her in the unique landscape of the Galápagos.

What is astonishing is the density and the variety. Many come well prepared: they have read, some have even studied. But all are struck by the nature that runs through its catalog unstintingly and unreservedly. Also on the east coast of Española, but on the other side of the island in Gardner Bay, you land on a beach where scores of sea lions (*Zalophus californianus*) doze, positioned with their pups between sand and dunes. Among the infinite strategies of nature, sea lions' excrement feeds sea iguanas (*Amblyrhynchus cristatus*): prehistoric reptiles that can swim while holding their breath thanks to their ability to reduce their heart rate to a minimum. Around them, there are extremely elegant crabs, *Grapsus grapsus*, with a red and yellow carapace, which move on the cliffs

ADVICE FOR TRAVELERS

WHEN TO GO They are on the Equator, but they have a mild subtropical climate, with temperatures fluctuating between 59 and 86 °F. The best season to visit them is the dry season, from June to November: the sea is calm and the water is more transparent, suitable for snorkeling and diving.

HOW TO GET THERE There are flights from Quito and Guayaquil. Individual trips are prohibited to protect the environment. You can only visit the islands on small ships (maximum 100 passengers) and sailboats.

WHAT YOU NEED Hiking shoes, sunglasses, hat, swimsuit, mask and flippers for snorkeling, binoculars for watching animals.

DIFFICULTIES Excursions are always accompanied by guides authorized by the marine park, who expect the visitors' behavior to conform to strict rules.

WEB SITES
www.discovergalapagos.com
www.darwinfoundation.org

covered with intensely green algae. Pelicans float lazily on the waves, while by night the giant tortoises (*Chelonoidis niger*) that have given their name to the archipelago – *galápago* in Spanish means "giant tortoise" – lay their eggs on this beach, digging holes in the sand. Once these marine reptiles were numerous on all the Galápagos beaches, but when at the end of the eighteenth century the whalers replaced the pirates in the archipelago, about 200,000 tortoises were killed for their meat, and the local seals were hunted for the precious fur, leading the tortoises to almost complete extinction.

After the incredible meeting with scores of creatures, there are more to be seen by snorkeling in the crystalline seas of Gardner Bay: it is another "intimate" experience with nature. You do not swim among corals and tropical fish as in other pacific archipelagos, but face to face with sea lions, iguanas, penguins, mantas, hammerheads, and dolphins.

The blue seas of Darwin Bay, at Isla Genovesa, with white sand and black rocks, are the best setting to see the courtship rituals of the frigate birds: to attract the female, the male inflates the red pouch on his neck.

208 In the wild, the giant tortoises of the Galápagos on average live 100 years, while in captivity they can live almost twice that.

209 Two blue-footed boobies: during courtship, the males display their bright blue feet to attract the females.

And the rituals of the sulas, which flirt in a spectacular ritual after building their nest on alternating layers of branches and guano. When the guides relate the habits of these birds – but also of iguanas, tortoises, sea lions, albatrosses and storm petrels – they combine scientific information and romanticized scenes of seduction. Their tales are a compromise between a naturalist's introduction and a soap opera. It must be so in the Galápagos, given that they are in South America: 13 volcanic islands scattered in the Pacific Ocean, 745 miles from the coast of Ecuador. The landscape is semi-arid, the vegetation consists almost entirely of acacias, cacti and euphorbias.

Regarding the density and concentration of nature, each island has a characteristic element. On Isla Santa María, better known as Floreana, you go ashore at Punta Cormorant among black hills with scattered white tree trunks and you skirt a lagoon inhabited by pink flamingos. On the other side of the island you see penguins and sea lions.

Lagoons, basalt rocks, and mangrove forests distinguish the landscape of Fernandina, at the foot of the youngest volcano in the archipelago. Here and on nearby Isabela there are active volcanoes. The Galápagos, situated in the Pacific ring of fire, have experienced 50 eruptions in the last 200 years. Here, when you land at Punta Espinoza, there are close encounters with marine iguanas, important in Darwin's theory of evolution. Quite often you spot a mother whale and her calf on the horizon in the channel

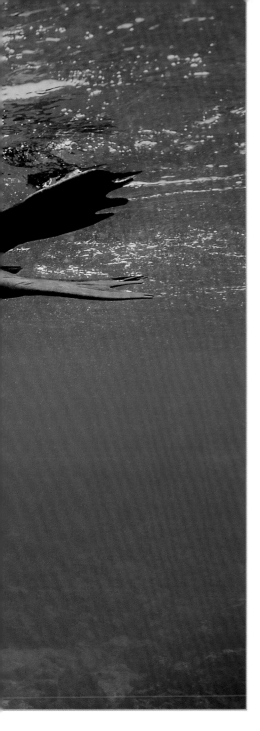

dividing Fernandina and Isabela. It is dawn, and rosy light colors the sky with enchanting shades of pastel. All the passengers are on deck armed with binoculars and cameras. This can become the most moving moment of the trip: the meeting with the giants of the sea which, while always moving delicately, because of their size create waves and currents.

When you land at Tagus Cove, on Isabela, a one-mile path leads to the lip of the crater holding a salt lake, to enjoy the spectacular view of the channel separating it from Fernandina; the rest of the island is desolate, with the cones of volcanoes alternating with lava fields and areas of tree trunks calcified by the drought, together with the occasional cactus. However, the best postcard from the island is Bartolomé: you climb the peak to admire the effect of beaches, mountains, sea stacks, and pinnacles below. Between one excursion and the next, most evenings you anchor at Santa Cruz, the capital and main center. The cruise ends at San Cristóbal, but the surprises do not: you could come across a couple of sea lions lying under the bus for the airport. Assuming almost an hour to make them move, you could arrive just in time not to miss the plane.

210-211 Two young sea lions play in the water.

211 top Encounter with a whale shark, the largest in the world but harmless to man.

211 bottom The small Galápagos penguin is the only species of this family to live in the tropical area.

212-213 The marine iguana, a prehistoric reptile with bizarre characteristics, is the only known example of sea lizard.

THE ORIGIN OF THE THEORY OF EVOLUTION

The extraordinary fauna of the Galápagos fascinated Charles Darwin, who explored the archipelago during his five-year circumnavigation of the world on the brigantine (1831-1836) HMS Beagle. Here the British scientist found the elements to formulate his theory of evolution, which revolutionized scientific thought. In his diary The Voyage of the "Beagle" *Darwin dedicated 26 pages to the Galápagos, describing the unique species encountered here, the tortoises of over 220 pounds that have given their name to the archipelago, the lizards up to 3 feet long. Darwin discovered that the majority of the animal and vegetable species on each island were endemic: they lived only here, because isolation had originated a different evolution.*

On the island of Santa Cruz the Charles Darwin Research Station continues the research begun two centuries ago by the British scientist. The station is in the center of a cactus forest on the seashore and holds, in special enclosures, enormous sea turtles and land iguanas (Conolophus subcristatus). *Here the researchers study the evolution of the fauna, but also monitor possible environmental damage caused by tourism with over 100,000 visitors per year. In fact, the archipelago has become one of the most popular eco-tourist destinations, a top destination for bird-watching, whale-watching, and to see unusual and bizarre plants and animals. The Galápagos – a* UNESCO *World Heritage Site – are one of the most important biodiversity reserves on the planet and the second marine reserve after the Australian Great Barrier Reef.*

BOLIVIA

THE MIRAGE OF SALT

THE SALAR DE UYUNI, IN BOLIVIA, IS THE INANIMATE
WORLD, THE MINERAL WORLD, AND THE WORLD
OF THE COLOR WHITE. AMONG OTHER THINGS,
IT ALSO REPRESENTS A UNIQUE EXPERIENCE FOR
TRAVELERS, WITH UNEXPECTED ENCOUNTERS WITH
AREAS OF CACTI AND COLONIES OF FLAMINGOS.

It is perhaps the most alien of the world's deserts; a place where you lose every spatial-temporal coordinate and are overwhelmed by an endless fascination; a place where it is easy to get lost. Paradoxically, this salt desert, completely unsuitable for human survival, is one of the most popular destinations in Bolivia: the Salar de Uyuni can easily be reached by plane from La Paz or in a day by car. But once it is reached, you immediately find extreme conditions: an altitude of 12,000 feet, night temperatures that can reach -4 °F, a reflection more dazzling than that of a glacier.

214-215 A convoy of 4x4s crosses the Salar de Uyuni in the rainy season. Only vehicles specifically prepared to withstand the corrosive action of salt can venture into this desert.

215 Cycling across the Salar, formed from about 11 salt layers between 6 and 33 feet thick.

MINERAL RESERVE

Sodium, chlorine, boron, potassium, magnesium, lithium: the Salar reserve is estimated at 10 billion tons. In practice, it is an inexhaustible reserve of salts, particularly lithium, which is a basic element of batteries for electronic devices. It is estimated that the Salar contains at least a third of the world's lithium, which is also easily obtainable. This means it is a great resource for Bolivia and also a predestined victim of industry.

And a perfectly uniform horizon, with no reference point, which prompts you to do the excursion only accompanied by expert guides. The Salar extends for 4,000 square miles in an area occupied in a former era by an immense lake. On its edges, the great Andean volcanoes rise, like Tunupa, on the north bank, 17,457 feet of oxidized rock in every shade of red, whose summit seasoned walkers can reach.

According to the Quechua legend, a son was born from the relationship between Yana Pollera (the maternal mountain) and Tunupa. He was, however, claimed by another lover, the volcano Q'osho. To distance the child from the feud, Yana Pollera sent him far away, and to nourish him she flooded the valley with her milk, mixed with the salt of her tears.

Thus the Salar was formed; today it has the appearance of an endless

WHEN TO GO The Salar de Uyuni can be visited throughout the year: the ideal period is between August and October, between the end of the southern winter and the beginning of the rainy season.

HOW TO GET THERE You reach the mining city of Uyuni, from where the excursions leave for Salar, by bus, by plane (three flights a week) or by 4X4 from La Paz along the n.1 road, via Oruro.

WHAT YOU NEED It is indispensable to take thermal clothing suitable for high altitudes and low temperatures, sunblock cream with a high protection factor, ice glasses, and trekking boots. A winter sleeping bag is useful, whether you take a trip of three days, and sleep in a tent (equipped for low temperatures) or in hostels (there is even a hotel built out of salt blocks).

DIFFICULTIES The trip is made in 4X4s, with brief excursions on foot. In the Salar, you can easily lose your sense of direction: it is therefore highly advisable to be guided by one of the numerous travel agencies in Uyuni.

WEB SITES
www.visitbolivia.org
boliviatravelsite.com
www.palaciodesal.com.bo
www.uyunitoursbolivia.com

ice-covered lake: white and solid in the dry season, when the surface seems to form regular hexagons, and shining in the rainy season, when it is covered by a film of water reflecting the sky. It is the moment when the Salar is transformed into the largest lake in the world. Everything is doubled before your eyes, from the Great Bear to the sun appearing behind the clouds.

You can "try" the Salar with day excursions; but you live when you can breathe the night, with your tents pitched beside the jeep. Dawn and sunset are always spectacular and you see everything of the starry firmament, down to the smallest one in the sky.

There is some life here: forests of cacti grow on the islands within the Salar de Uyuni, especially the Isla Incahuasi and the Isla del Pescado, where archeological remains can be found of the Incas and the Tiahuanaco civilization. And in the lagoons around the Salar, which are full of red algae, as many as three species of flamingo come to breed.

The sight of pink flocks on the blinding expanse of salt is one of the strangest and most unforgettable spectacles on the planet.

216 The Laguna Colorada, on the edge of the Salar de Uyuni. The algae reddening its waters are food for the flamingos that come here to breed.

217 top The sunset is mirrored on the Salar. According to Inca legends, in the desert you can find the *ojos de Salar*, cavities on the surface that are difficult to spot: they swallowed up caravans of unsuspecting travelers.

217 bottom In winter, the crystallizations on the surface of the Salar form a pattern as far as the eye can see.

CHILE

ATACAMA, THE MOST ARID WORLD

A LUNAR LANDSCAPE FORMED OF STONY PLANES,
CANYONS, AND PINNACLES. SUNBURNED EXPANSES
THAT THE VERY RARE RAINS CAUSE TO SPROUT.
BUT EVEN THE GEYSER PLATEAUS AND SALT LAKES
INHABITED BY THOUSANDS OF FLAMINGOS,
WHERE WATER HOLDS SWAY.

It is the most arid desert on the planet, with just 20 mm of precipitation per year.
Such a dry climate has preserved extraordinary geological formations, natural
sculptures formed by the wind over thousands of years. Straddling the Tropic of
Capricorn, in the north of Chile, the Atacama Desert is a rock plateau that can

218 The *Mano del desierto* is a sculpture 36 feet high completed in 1992 by the Chilean artist Mario
Irarrázabal, 46 miles from the city of Antofagasta.

218-219 "Extraterrestrial" dawn in the geothermic area of El Tatio, the largest geyser field on the planet.

ADVICE FOR TRAVELERS

WHEN TO GO Throughout the year. Average summer temperatures fluctuate between 81 and 6 °F, with more marked temperature differences in winter (between 72 and 39 °F).

HOW TO GET THERE The airport of reference is Calama, 61 miles from San Pedro de Atacama, with regular flights for Santiago.

WHAT YOU NEED Light clothing in cotton or natural fibers, light hiking shoes, hat, sunglasses.

DIFFICULTIES Don't forget the altitude: at 13,000 feet you breathe less oxygen and you must move more carefully.

WEB SITES
sanpedroatacama.com
chile.travel/en/where-to-go/
north-and-the-atacama-desert

220 top The expanse of the Laguna Leja, in which the impressive Lascar volcano is mirrored.

220 bottom The Laguna Cejar is an emerald pool in the middle of the desert. Floating is facilitated enormously by the high salt concentration.

221 An aerial view of the pinnacled scenery of the Valle de Marte (also called Valle de La Muerte).

exceed 13,000 feet in altitude; it extends for 41,000 square miles, the entire size of Bulgaria.

The almost total absence of rain ensures that the Atacama sky is one of the clearest on the planet, of a blue the same intensity as the ochre of the desert. It is a magical place in which the visitor is transformed – according to the moment – into an explorer, astronomer, botanist, or birdwatcher. Due to the clarity of the sky, Atacama has been chosen for the installation of some of the most important astronomical observatories in the world: here, it is extraordinary to look up at the night sky. And NASA, the aerospace agency of the United States, has used it several times to test the technological efficiency of robots and vehicles for lunar and Martian landings and research. The exceptional rain that takes place every five or six years creates a thrilling spectacle: the "flowering desert." About 200 autochthonous species germinate, among which are some in danger of extinction, millions of delicate petals that create surprising colored carpets– intense purple, white and yellow, lavender, lilac and fiery red.

In a 4X4 you can explore gorges, rocky plains, sand dunes, and salt formations which together create a triumphant extraterrestrial landscape in

the Valle de la Luna, 9 miles from San Pedro de Atacama. Here, the houses are made of adobe (bricks of dried clay, sand and straw), with pinnacles and rocks covered with salt crystals that reflect white and pink. You feel even more like a pioneer if you continue northeast, where you find the spectacular canyons of Valle de Marte e Cordillera de la Sal.

About 60 miles north of San Pedro, the desolation of the desert gives way to the geothermic area of El Tatio, the largest geyser field on Earth, with approximately one hundred water jets at a temperature of 176 °F, sometimes reaching more than 30 feet in height.

On the way to El Tatio you can stop at Termas de Puritama to bathe in the hot water springs. South of San Pedro, nature still plays with water: there is the enormous Salar de Atacama, the largest salt lake in Chile (1,200 square miles), where the light penetrates the crystals, giving the illusion of an expanse of water. In the Laguna Chaxa you are transformed into a birdwatcher: it is tinted pink by thousands of flamingos that, in this surreal scenery, survive thanks to algae and microorganisms. While if you dive into the Laguna Cejar, you float better than on the Dead Sea because of the density of lithium in its waters.

THE MIRAGE OF THE MARBLE CAVES

ONE OF THE MOST SURPRISING NATURAL SPECTACLES
IN PATAGONIA CONSISTS OF THE MARBLE GROTTOES
FORMED BY EROSION AND COLORED BY WATER,
LIGHT AND ICE IN INFINITE VARIATIONS.

A Chilean legend relates that when God had finished creating the wonders of the earth, there were many pieces left over: parts of rivers and deserts, glaciers and forests, pieces of mountains and green meadows. To ensure that they were not lost, He put them together and created Chile. When you admire the beauty and, above all, the variety of Chilean landscapes you are forced to believe the ancient legend. And the Marble Caves – a mosaic composed of lake water, marble, ice and sunbeams are definitely no exception.

222 The spectacular entrance to one of the grottoes of the system, called Marble Cathedral, a natural monument threatened today by the attempt to begin new building on the lake.

222-223 The base of the *stack*, which rises in the center of the branches of Lake Carrera, can easily be reached in a kayak and is not far from the shore.

224-225 The geological marvel of the marble grottoes, the door to the center of the earth, is most appealing when the water level is lower. The lake is fed by melt-waters from glaciers.

225 The spectacle continues beneath the water, whose transparency also enables you to admire the submerged formations.

ADVICE FOR TRAVELERS

WHEN TO GO The southern autumn (from April to June) is the best season to visit the Marble Chapels because the low water level allows the warm light of dawn and sunset to penetrate them. In summer (from December to February) the high water does not offer this spectacle, but the grottoes are completely illuminated.

HOW TO GET THERE You fly from Santiago to Balmaceda, from where you drive for about 186 miles along the Carretera Austral (an unpaved road) as far as Puerto Río Tranquilo, the base for the Marble Chapels excursions.

WHAT YOU NEED It can also be cold in summer, with low temperatures around 44 °F: don't forget to take a windproof jacket, fleece, hat, gloves, trekking shoes, sunglasses, and sunblock cream.

DIFFICULTIES Accessible to everyone.

WEB SITES marmolexpediciones.cl, chile.travel, news.southamerica.travel

Lying on the southern Andes, at an altitude of 712 feet, General Carrera Lake is about 714 square miles in area.

At its center, the meeting point of three branches, we find the Marble Caves, one of the most bizarre geological formations on the planet.

During an excursion in a small boat, taking at the most ten people, the first thing you see is the stack, a monolith that water and ice have shaped into an immense mushroom. It is an example of the marvels you find when the boat enters the grottoes (even though the best means to enter them is a kayak), where a thousand years of erosion have carved true masterpieces in marble. In 6,000 years, the waves of the Andean lake have created a series of tunnels and chambers with curved walls, supported by columns that seem to be bundles of sugar paste; caves penetrated by the light of the sun, where the marble is transformed into a kaleidoscope. The walls are streaked with blue and turquoise, reflections of sapphire and smoky gray, and aquamarine, white, yellowish and cerulean colors, which change over the year according to the level of the water. The lake is fed by a glacier and it is just the glacial silt that gives the marble the range of blues that dominates over the other colors.

While the sun's rays modify the forms on the rocks and the shade effects in each season, the water level changes the intensity of the blue on the walls: a crescendo that ranges from sky to dark blue.

When the boat enters the two largest grottoes, called – imaginatively – the Marble Chapel and the Marble Cathedral, you feel as if you're living in a fairy tale: deep in the crystalline waters, you can see other blue and green rock formations, other allure.

ARGENTINA

ADVENTURES ON THE GLACIER AT THE END OF THE WORLD

PERPETUAL MOVEMENT, GIANT PINNACLES, DAZZLING COLORS ARE THE BEST KNOWN ASPECTS OF THE PERITO MORENO, IN THE HEART OF THE PATAGONIAN ANDES. IT IS A NOBLE GLACIER WORTHY OF YOUR RESPECT: IN COMPLETE SAFETY WEARING CRAMPONS, OR FROM THE SPECIALLY EQUIPPED BANKS OF ARGENTINO LAKE.

226-227   The Perito Moreno is part of the continental glacier, Campo de Hielo Patagónico Sur, between Chile and Argentina.

227   The front of the Perito Moreno is 2.5 miles wide and extends for 32 miles on Argentino Lake. It literally creates a dam between the two arms of the lake, so that the water level of Brazo Rico can rise more than 98 feet above the usual level.

WHEN TO GO The southern summer lasts from December to March; January is to be avoided, because in Argentina it is the most crowded and expensive vacation period.

HOW TO GET THERE El Calafate is served by an international airport. Daily flights connect it to Buenos Aires in about 3 hours. From the city Argentino Lake can be reached by car in an hour and a half along provincial road 15, or by bus lines.

WHAT YOU NEED Temperatures can also be low in summer, with very windy days and sudden precipitation. It is essential to have waterproof thermal clothing and hiking shoes. If you go on an excursion on the glacier, you need to wear heavy, crampon-fitted boots. These are supplied by the guides, together with the ice axes.

DIFFICULTIES Possible for everyone: the hikes on the glacier are accessible even for those with no climbing experience; the gangways are level and well protected.

WEB SITES
www.argentina.travel
www.patagonia-argentina.com
www.hieloyaventura.com
glaciarium.com

Campo de Hielo Patagónico Sur, one of the most extensive ice caps in the world, represents one of the last examples of true wilderness and is the goal of climbers and travelers. It is still partly unexplored, and subject to the Patagonian winds, in the unpredictable oceanic climate. It covers 6,500 square miles, and 49 glaciers converge on it: it touches legendary mountains like Cerro Torre, Fitz Roy, Torres del Paine,

and several national parks, among which Los Glaciares, since 1981 a Unesco World Heritage site.

It is in this park that the most popular and most photographed glacier flows: Perito Moreno. It terminates its 18 mile-long course in the southernmost branch of Argentino Lake, which divides it in two by a powerful dam of seracs.

Named after Francisco Moreno, an Argentinian explorer and anthropologist

228 Hikers on the Perito Moreno pass small lagoons, deep fissures, ice formations, streams and gullies.

229 top The boat is the best way to appreciate the majesty of the ice walls.

229 bottom A *mirador*, a wooden boardwalk, is a lookout point *par excellence*.

230 A great freshwater reservoir, seen from above the Perito Moreno, has the shape of a tongue of ice, advancing at the speed of almost half mile per year.

231 The pressure of the lake provokes loud explosions of ice calving along the ice barrier. Preceded by a roar, the blocks of ice can create very dangerous waves. For this reason, boats must maintian a safe distance.

who first discovered the lake at the end of the 19th century (without ever reaching the glacier, however), today it is a destination that is as easy to reach as it is spectacular.

The seracs are a gigantic wall of towers and pinnacles of pale blue ice, which contrasts with the dark shades of the water and the intense green of the woods surrounding the lake.

In the long days of the southern summer, the front of the perpetually advancing glacier really puts on a show, which the visitors keenly try to capture with their cameras: large and small fragments of ice, but also entire pillars up to 200 feet high, break away from the seracs and plunge into the water with a stunning splash. The remains of these collapses then continue to float in the lake, like icebergs with fantastical eroded forms. The climax of the spectacle is the collapse of the grotto dug into the ice dam by water pressure,

in the so-called *zona de ruptura*, between Argentino Lake and Brazo Rico: periodically the entire vault collapses, enabling the two sections of the lake to communicate again.

Of all the glaciers in the world, Perito Moreno is one of the most vital: it is apparently immune to the effects of global warming (even though glaciologists have detected a loss of thickness in the last few years). It continues to advance by 6.5 feet a day, as shown by the continual creaking from its surface, and then loses the same distance due to collapses. It is a guaranteed spectacle for the approximately 100,000 visitors who venture to the banks of the lake every year.

You can reach the lake rapidly, by car or by coach, from the Argentinian city of El Calafate, 48 miles away; from the Magallanes peninsular, where the road ends. From here the more adventurous go into the forest, until

they reach the glacier; a really remarkable sight of crevices, cracks, crests and pinnacles sculpted into the blue ice, which now European glaciers, battered by Global warming, no longer present.

With the guides and wearing crampons, two hikes are available: one lasting an hour and a half, and the other three hours and a half, on the tormented surface of Perito Moreno, listening to the creaking of the ice as it advances unnoticeably, like a slow river, and the sound of the water from melted ice at the bottom of the crevices.

If you want to see the spectacle of "calving," which means the collapse of the seracs into the lake from the glacier front, you should leave the parking lot and walk onto the wood and metal gangways, a system of colored pathways that lead to lookout points. They are always quite near to the glacier front, but at a safe distance from the collapses (owing to accidents in the past, it is prohibited to come closer to the seracs). Besides the great surrounding scenery (the snowy Andes, the lake, Perito Moreno fracturing with the dramatic splashes), the sounds of the cracking glacier and the wind are the protagonists of the experience.

It takes at most three hours to walk around the gangways: it is better in the afternoon, when there are fewer visitors and the higher temperatures encourage the breaking away of the ice. Tourist agencies in El Calafate offer day-long excursions on Argentino Lake, on a boat or in a kayak, to admire the front of the seracs from the water. But before stepping onto the glacier, it is very interesting to visit the local museum, Glaciarium, with its scenic architecture and focus on the secret life of the Patagonian glaciers.

HAWAII ●

BIG ISLAND: FIRE AND GARLANDS OF FLOWERS

VISITING VOLCANOES ALONG THE CHAIN OF CRATERS ROAD ON THE ISLAND OF HAWAII, WALKING IN A PETRIFIED LAVA FLOW, FLYING OVER THE ERUPTING VOLCANO'S MOUTH, WATCHING A RED RIVER FLOWING INTO THE OCEAN. ALL THIS HAPPENS IN THE MIDDLE OF THE PACIFIC, FAR AWAY FROM THE REST OF THE WORLD.

Resting in the blue Pacific Ocean, more than 2,000 miles from the West Coast of the US, Hawaii has always been a world in itself. Of about 150 islands emerging from the Pacific, only seven are inhabited. The oldest islands, in the northwestern extremity of the chain, have now been reduced to simple coral atolls by sea erosion. In contrast, the opposite extremity is characterized by

large islands with high mountains and significant volcanic activity. Oahu is the most populous, with over 80% of the total population. On this island we find Honolulu, the capital, and Pearl Harbor.

The largest island is Hawaii, called the Big Island for this reason: its surface area is more than half that of the entire archipelago. Its main feature is the twin volcanoes, more than 13,000 feet high,

which dominate the landscape and control its climate. Their slopes plunge into the Pacific Ocean for 19,000 feet, which means deep seas, no coral reefs, and enormous waves.

232 Lava flowing out of the crater Puu Oo, one of the numerous mouths of Kilauea, which has been continuously active since 1983.

233 Kilauea erupting. Hawai'i, or the "Big Island," is the largest in the Hawaiian archipelago. It grows by 42 acres a year due to the continuous eruptions.

234 Hawaiian myths relate that the goddess Pele, the custodian of fire and the volcano, lives in fiery magma. The goddess may take the form of a lovely woman or a very old one: she is always looking for a perfect fiery refuge.

235 Magma pours into the Pacific Ocean. Punaluu Beach, on the south coast of Big Island, is the result of constant volcanic and oceanic activity, which has made the sand a shiny black.

 ## ADVICE FOR TRAVELERS

WHEN TO GO Throughout the year: the temperatures are very high, between 75 and 84 °F. The rainiest season is between October and November.

HOW TO GET THERE By plane (about 5 hours), from the US/Canadian west coast. Frequent flights from Los Angeles, San Francisco, Seattle and Vancouver.

WHAT YOU NEED Summer clothing, good shoes with thick soles, an insulated jacket or fleece if you want to reach the summit of Mauna Kea.

DIFFICULTIES Accessible to everyone.

WEB SITES www.gohawaii.com, www.govisithawaii.com, www.hawaii.com/travel/visitor-info

Due to its continuously active volcanoes, the Big Island is one of the best places in the world to get close to molten or petrified lava.

To start with, you can get an idea of the landscape by helicopter. Scenic flights take off from several heliports to follow volcanic activity. Sometimes you can see explosive eruptions with jets of lava expelled from the volcanoes' mouths, while sometimes red rivers flow toward the sea. Those called "skylights" are amazing: windows in the solid lava

236 Kilauea is the only volcano on the planet whose summit can be reached by car; it can be explored on 150 miles of paths in the park.

237 Lava entering the ocean generates vast clouds of steam. In some cases, when the lava temperature is much higher than normal, contact with cold ocean water provokes an explosion of steam that is so violent that it hurls debris and rocks for hundreds of feet.

crust, which allow you to glimpse the fiery magma flow under the surface.

Another really exciting viewpoint to see lava is from the sea. You reach the most active area by a powerful launch (because proximity to magma is always dangerous, it is essential to rely on experienced operators). The spectacle is breathtaking: here nature flexes her muscles. The rivulets of lava flowing into the sea explode when they meet the water, creating enormous vapor clouds. Dusk is the time both for boat and for helicopter observation: the less the daylight, the redder the lava.

You can have other close and intimate encounters with the beating heart of the island by car or on foot. The panoramic roads covering Hawaii are among the most beautiful in the world; they enable you to discover both the coasts and the interior. The Kohala Coast, arid and marked by enormous lava flows, extends north of Kailua for about 31 miles. South of Kailua, the Kona Cost is completely different. The road winds between palms, along small inlets and close to cultivated fields.

Just a few miles separates Kailua from Kealakekua Bay, where, apart from the black sand, there is a monument to Captain Cook. The famous navigator was killed on this shore on February 14th, 1779 upon his second voyage to Hawaii.

Not far way, we find the Pu'uhonua O Hōnaunau National Historical Park, known as the Place of Refuge, a sacred and very evocative place. You continue through a lush region, with many coffee and macadamia plantations (the latter is an extremely tasty nut native to these islands). Passing the

southern point of the island, you reach the Punaluʻu Black Sand Beach Park, a splendid black lava beach fringed by palms with a small lagoon behind. The black sand is produced by the explosion of red lava in contact with the ocean. Erosion destroys these beaches rapidly (in geological time). For now, Punaluʻu Black Sandy Beach is in very good health and the contrast between the black, the turquoise of the sea, and the green of the palms constitutes a matchless spectacle.

From here, Highway 11 starts to climb and you reach the realm of Pele, the goddess who lives atop the volcanoes, by entering the Hawaii Volcanoes National Park by the winding Chain of Craters Road, which is considered by many to be one of the most beautiful roads in the world. The route is amazing, moving from one crater to another, from one lava flow to the

next. Often you can get close enough to the red-hot magma to touch it with a stick.

You need at least a couple of days to visit the Hawaii Volcanoes National Park. Don't miss a visit to Thurston Lava Tubes – where it is possible to walk inside an old lava flow that has made a series of tunnels – and go on an excursion along the Devastation Trail that crosses a particularly spectacular series of flows. To approach the red lava, you should arrange the visit with the park rangers monitoring its activity.

Usually, it is possible to follow marked trails leading to the point where the lava enters the sea; or to reach particularly slow and less scorching flows that you can approach to within a few inches. It is not rare to come across roads closed by active flows, or travel along roads blocked by now-solidified lava flows.

HAWAII ●

WALKING IN THE PAINTED FOREST

IN THE MAUI RAIN FOREST, IN THE MIDDLE
OF THE PACIFIC OCEAN, THERE GROW MAJESTIC TREES
WITH A COLORFUL BARK: A RAINBOW PLANT.

There is a tree that changes its clothes every day of the year, donning a phantasmagorical variety of colors: it is the *Eucalyptus deglupta*, the only species of eucalyptus that grows naturally in the Northern Hemisphere.

On Maui, the most luxuriant Hawaiian island, they call it the Rainbow Eucalyptus; here thickets, rows or isolated trees, which are often colossal (the height can reach 230 feet, the trunk diameter 6.5 feet) are a real tourist attraction, an easy destination for

trekkers who venture into the rain forest. When they come across one, towering among hibiscus, giant ferns and bamboo thickets, they cannot help but stop to admire and photograph it.

However, it is the bark, not the foliage, that makes the show: the old bark peels away continuously in long strips, revealing bright green wood.

The wood changes color with time and oxidation, through blue, purple, orange and brown: flamboyant, continually-evolving motifs form.

The best moment to catch the various colors is after the rain (which in the rainforest, is frequent), when the clothing of the *Eucalyptus deglupta* is most brilliant and gives off a strong scent of balsam. It is an experience for the nose as well as for the eyes.

238 The multicolor bark of the *Eucalyptus deglupta*. Strips of bark fall and reveal the bare wood, whose color in time changes from bright green to orange, to blue, to purple.

239 A tropical moth is camouflaged on the bark.

 ## ADVICE FOR TRAVELERS

WHEN TO GO Hawaii's climate is tropical, with average temperatures fluctuating between 66 and 87 °F. The hottest and driest months are from December to March; the east coasts exposed to the trade winds are generally cooler and rainier.

HOW TO GET THERE Kahului airport has daily connections with the other islands and major US cities. The flight from Honolulu lasts forty-five minutes.

WHAT YOU NEED For walks in the rainforest you need light, breathable clothing, hiking shoes and, in the Hana area, mosquito repellent. Don't forget your swimsuit for a dip in the waterfalls.

DIFFICULTIES The excursions are all simple, without too much difference in altitude or problems of orientation, but to find the painted woods and the best waterfalls immediately it is better to hire a guide. Many tours in the Hana parks are organized directly from the hotels.

WEB SITES haleakalaranch.com, www.gohawaii.com

There are various localities in Maui where it is easy to admire the eucalyptus trees: like the Haleakala Ranch, one of the oldest and most extensive in the Hawaiian islands, on the Crater Road (State Highway 378) for the Haleakala National Park.

The ranch, at 4,200 feet, was also the first place where the Rainbow Eucalyptus was transplanted from its home in the Philippines at the beginning of the twentieth century: its rapidly-growing wood (the trees can grow up to 16 feet in a year) was meant to be used as fuel for the sugar cane industry.

Today, you can find it in thickets scattered over the ranch, and its colors are visible for miles. You can begin an enjoyable eco-adventure from the visitors' center, combining an excursion on foot with seven zip lines that run among the eucalyptus woods. On the zip line, the movement transforms the colored bark into multicolored lines that dance faster and faster before your eyes.

The painted forest on the east coast of Maui is still easier to see, lying along the Hana Highway, 60 miles of spectacular road (declared a national monument). Its links the towns of Kahului and Hana and crosses the parks of Kaumahina and Wai'anapanapa, which are dotted with waterfalls, rainforest paths, and wide views of the coast. Here you only need to park the car and walk for a few steps to meet the most multicolored tree in the world.

240-241 A eucalyptus rises among the philodendrons. These trees are not native to Hawaii: they were imported for the high quality of the wood, also used in building and paper production.

241 Rainbow eucalyptuses along the Hana Highway, on the east coast of Maui. These trees are the only eucalyptuses growing spontaneously in the northern hemisphere.

POLYNESIA ●

SAILING TO THE MARQUESAS ISLANDS

THE WILDEST, MOST REMOTE ARCHIPELAGO
OF POLYNESIA IS A MYTHICAL DESTINATION
FOR SKIPPERS: IT FEATURES VOLCANIC
HORIZONS AND BAYS WITH THE SCENT
OF DELICATE FRANGIPANI.

On the bows appear steep mountains and basalt peaks shrouded in clouds.
They are the Marquesas Islands, the easternmost and most isolated archipelago in
the Pacific Ocean. There are twelve islands, only half of them inhabited. Specks in the
southern seas, they were formed by ancient volcanoes and lie along an axis of
186 miles, northeast of Tahiti on the long route toward Hawaii. They are harsh lands:
their position straddling the Equator, with a fiery climate, makes them inhospitable.

    They are the furthest islands from the Polynesia of our imagination: there are

242-243   The steep cliffs of Fatu Hiva, whose verticality is due to the volcanic origin of the island.

243   Pointed volcanic summits form the profile of the island of Ua Pou. The Marquesas Islands present
a dramatic landscape, harsh and furrowed, very far from the seaside image of Polynesia.

neither lagoons nor coral reefs. But they form a mythical archipelago for sailing enthusiasts, who - after the flat atolls of the Tuamotu Islands and the monotony of days on the open sea - finally see the blue horizon turn black, ochre, and green. The black is the volcanoes, the ochre the sandy beaches, the green a dense rainforest, blanketed by waterfalls, as at Nuku Hiva.

You first land at Hiva Oa, where you moor in Atuona Bay, dominated by the 3,979 feet of the volcano Temetiu. It is the island of *recherche sauvage*, the last dwelling of Paul Gauguin, who came here

"to be immersed in virgin nature and share the life of the savages." The *poète maudit* rests in the shade of the frangipani, in the tiny Calvary Cemetery, from which you can enjoy a splendid view of Atuona Bay. Sailing northward, you coast the arid Ua Huka, on whose cliffs millions of sooty terns (*Onychoprion fuscatus*) nest. Nuku Hiva, the main island, lies further to the north. The safe landing is in Taioha'e Bay, which is surrounded by a chain of peaks with bizarre forms. Covered with vegetation, they seem to be sentinels guarding the sea.

Herman Melville lived for a month in 1842 in the parallel valley of Taipivai. In the novel *Taipi*, this was the setting of a story of cannibals who practiced human sacrifice and carved *tiki*, the anthropomorphic figures of divinities and ancestors. You can reach these wood or rock sculptures, which stand on megalithic platforms, in the archeological sites of the island, by trekking through the vapors of the sweltering jungle.

You need to circumnavigate Nuku Hiva to discover the different expressions of the sublime: stony bays dominated by

WHEN TO GO The dry season, from November to April, is the best period: the climate is less sultry. The rains, from May to October, are not torrential, but make an already humid climate even more oppressive.

HOW TO GET THERE By sailboat: the Marquesas lie 930 miles northeast of Tahiti and 2,500 miles south of Honolulu. By plane: Air Tahiti flies from Papeete to Nuku Hiva and Hiva Oa.

WHAT YOU NEED Shorts, T-shirts, sandals, hiking shoes, sunglasses, a hat with an insect face net, a swimsuit, insect repellent suitable for the jungle.

DIFFICULTIES Despite challenging climatic conditions, it is accessible to everyone.

WEB SITES
tahititourisme.org
www.tahiti.com
www.tahititravel.com.au

systems of pinnacles, alternating with high scarp cliffs, as in the bay of Hakaui, where a dizzying waterfall cuts through the mountain; or, on the north coast, Hatiheu Bay, enclosed by a rocky crown that casts a shadow on emerald green valleys, studded with millions of palms.

244 Two *tiki* survey Hatiheu Bay, along the north-western coast of Nuku Hiva.

245 top The Vaiea waterfall, on Ua Pou: in its natural pool you can safely refresh yourself.

245 center Aerial view of the island Nuku Hiva, the largest in the archipelago.

245 bottom The island of Fatu Hiva was discovered in 1595 by the Spanish explorer Alvaro de Mendana.

SWIMMING WITH WHALES

TO CELEBRATE THE MATING SEASON, THE HUMPBACK WHALES REACH THE WARM EQUATORIAL WATERS OF THE POLYNESIAN ARCHIPELAGO, ONE OF THE RARE PLACES WHERE YOU CAN DIVE IN THE SAME WATER AMONG THE LARGEST CETACEANS IN THE WORLD.

The hydrophone transmits groans, cries, and moans. It is the underwater microphone that brings the song of the humpback whales to the surface. The sounds go on for hours, interspersed with brief pauses to breathe. According to etiologists, they are emitted above all by males to attract females. The whales communicate among themselves and involuntarily with humankind; the whale-watching pilots identify the cetaceans' position by means of the hydrophone, above

246-247 and 247 A young humpback whale rests, sheltered by his mother: there is a very close relationship between mother and calf, who stay together for the entire first year, communicating in a language of imperceptible whispers.

248 A diver films a humpback whale: Tonga is one of the few countries in which it is possible to do this. In fact, the law permits swimming with whales, which is possible in the northern archipelagos of Ha'Hapai and Vava'u.

248-249 A majestic female swims with her calf, escorted by a male. The females can be recognized by their greater size (they weigh up to 25-30 tons) and the white of the underside and fins.

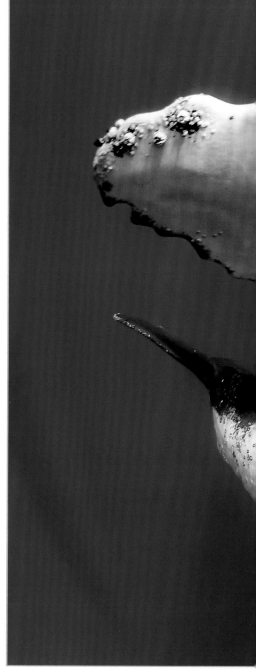

 ADVICE FOR TRAVELERS

WHEN TO GO The whale-watching season runs from July to October.

HOW TO GET THERE Tonga is served by Air New Zealand with daily flights from Auckland and by Virgin Australia with flights from Sydney. To see the humpback whales, you have to move from the main island of Tonga-tapu to the northern archipelagos of Ha'apai or Vava'u.

WHAT YOU NEED It is very hot: light casual clothing, shorts, undershirts, sandals, sunglasses, hat, swimming suit, mask and flippers.

DIFFICULTIES Do not underestimate the hot climate.

WEB SITES humpbackswims.com
www.tongaholiday.com/things-to-do/whale-watching

all in Tonga, in the central archipelago of Ha'apai – a universe of flat sandy islands, enclosed by coral reefs and turquoise seas: one of the few countries where the law allows swimming with whales.

Enchanted by the song of the humpback whales, you suddenly find yourself in the water, among all the shades of blue pierced by the rays of the sun that seem to plunge into the ocean depths. The whale does not disappoint: it arrives suddenly, not the least disturbed by human presence. Its great eye investigates the space. Its enormous head

breeches from the water, then it glides and falls back with a deafening splash. Its back is shiny: it's a female with a calf along her side. For a minute she swims just under the surface. Then she dives, disappearing into the depths and re-emerging after several minutes, as if she were playing hide-and-seek with the human beings swimming beside her, imperturbable in her armor of gentle steel. Respect for these giants of the sea is essential: you cannot come closer than 300 feet, silently, and must swim away at the first sign of irritation.

Humpback whales (*Megaptera novaeangliae*) have a prominent hump on their slate-gray backs. When they blow, the spout can reach 10 feet in height. They are from 39 to 55 feet long and weigh up to 40 tons: the females are generally longer than the males. They are powerful swimmers, using their enormous tail fin to propel them and assisted by pectoral fins along a third of their body. They spend the southern summer (December-March) in the icy, plankton-rich waters of the Antarctic. Then they migrate to reach the warm tropical seas

near the Equator during the southern winter (June-September) for the mating season, in a phenomenon that is repeated every year in various parts of the planet: extremely long migrations at 18 miles per hour in shallow seas.

They migrate in groups, and when possible near the coasts, alternating breeches with immersions 15-20 minutes long. After giving birth, mothers stay near their little ones for a year. We say "little," but at birth they measure 13 feet and weigh almost 1,500 pounds!

RIBBON REEF,
THE DIVERS' PARADISE

INTENSELY CRYSTALLINE AND TURQUOISE WATER,
WITH ONLY THE OCCASIONAL HUMAN PRESENCE.
SCORES OF NATIVE FISH SPECIES THAT BOLDLY
TWIRL AND LET THEMSELVES BE PHOTOGRAPHED.
IT IS THE SEA AS IT IS MEANT TO BE.

250-251 Aerial view of the Great Barrier Reef, off the Queensland coast. It extends over an area of over 130,000 square miles, and is even visible from space.

251 An immaculate beach along the northern coast of Lizard Island. The name of the island was chosen by James Cook during his first voyage in 1770. Upon arrival, it seemed to him to be inhabited only by one land animal, the lizard.

▶▶ ADVICE FOR TRAVELERS

WHEN TO GO The tropical climate encourages you to dive in every period of the year. The temperature of the water varies from 71 °F in winter to 84 °F in summer. Visibility is good throughout the year, but particularly so from September to November. The winter months (June-August) are the most suitable for diving, while the summer off-season is hotter and more humid, and much rainier.

HOW TO GET THERE Cairns International Airport (daily flights from Brisbane, Sydney, and Melbourne) is the most convenient way to reach the area. From Cairns and Port Douglas, there are daily excursions to the inner Great Barrier Reef and safari boat cruises to visit the outer reefs, like the Ribbon Reef.

WHAT YOU NEED Diving equipment is supplied by the excursion agencies; it is useful to carry your PADI diving certificate with you to demonstrate your experience.

DIFFICULTIES Suitable for divers and photographers of every level.

WEB SITES
www.mikeball.com
www.prodive-cairns.com.au
www.spiritoffreedom.com.au
www.lizardisland.com.au

◀◀

Ribbon Reef is a chain of 10 reefs extending for about 50 miles in the western part of the Great Barrier Reef. It is valued by scuba divers as one of the most beautiful places in the world for unspoiled nature, crystalline, transparent water and easy close encounters with the very many species that make up its great marine biodiversity. It is a remote place running along the northeast Australian coast, only accessible by boat. With little human activity nearby, it attracts very few visitors. It is unequalled for its beauty and exclusiveness.

Some areas are particularly well known to sea lovers: you must not miss Cod

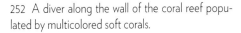

252 A diver along the wall of the coral reef populated by multicolored soft corals.

253 top and bottom The riches of these waters is unique. Scientists have reported the dramatic effects of global warming on delicate species like corals.

254-255 An *Epinephelus tukula*, a sociable giant grouper that can reach 6.5 feet in length.

255 A clown fish pops out curiously from the anemone that serves as its home: the two creatures have a symbiotic relationship.

Hole, the site famous for potato groupers (*Epinephelus tukula*), which fearlessly approach boats at mooring, and allow you to easily take spectacular photographs.

There are legends regarding the boldness of these groupers: it is said that it derives from this fish's habit of

obtaining food from passing ships.

The groupers are in good company: clown fishes, whitetip reef sharks, leopard morays, barracudas, and Napoleon wrasses (*Cheilinus undulatus*) with velvety, emerald-green scales.

On Lizard Island, there are endless

deserted beaches: it is a national park together with the surrounding smaller islands. You can have your fill of diving and snorkeling in the marvelous geometry of the coral barrier composed of pinnacles, walls and reefs.

Your most frequent encounters are with the local turtles, dolphins, dugongs and the pelagic fish. In summer, it is not uncommon to find yourself in the company of Minke whales (*Balaenoptera acutorostrata*).

Ribbon Reef is a paradise for every type of diver, with quite shallow areas (seldom do you swim below 65 feet) where it is possible to admire 1,500 species of fish and 400 types of coral. Day excursions are not possible, so to explore the seas sufficiently you need to stay at least three days. But after the first, it will be difficult to think of leaving.

NEW ZELAND

WAITOMO CAVES, THE UNDERGROUND STARLIT SKY

PLANETARIUM JOURNEY THROUGH FLUORESCENT GROTTOES
WITH STARRY COLORS, INHABITED BY BIOLUMINESCENT INSECTS,
THE PROTAGONISTS OF AN ASTOUNDING SPECTACLE.

The journey into the bowels of the earth is capable of astonishing even the most experienced travelers. The Waitomo grottoes present the world's most astonishing lightshow, due to the presence of small bioluminescent insects, glowworms (*Arachnocampa luminosa*) which form a veritable starry sky on the vault. These small creatures, resembling common mosquitoes, but larger (about 0.7 inches), only live in New Zealand; during the larval phase they emit rapid glows for a few moments to feed, just like fireflies. In fact, the larva produces a stringy web, about 20 inches long and dripping with saliva, which attracts its prey. If you watch it, however, it amplifies and reflects the glow, making everything increasingly iridescent. The light emitted by the insects varies from green to blue

256 Larvae of *Arachnocampa luminosa*, an endemic species to New Zealand, light up the vault of the grotto. In the Maori language, they are called *titiwai*, meaning "reflection on the water."

257 The webs of filament, up to 1 and a half feet long, contain a sticky serum that immobilizes their prey.

257

depending on their appetite . . . the hungrier they are the more they shine in the dark. In their larval period of nine months, these insects need a dark, humid place sheltered from the wind, and a ceiling to hang from. However, the life of an adult insect is short: only a few days.

Structured on three levels, the Waitomo Caves are thus the ideal habitat. You enter through the area called the Catacombs, formed of small pathways dug out of the rock, and then reach the Banquet Hall and finally the Cathedral, the biggest cave, whose name derives from an enormous limestone structure shaped like an organ.

The first men to explore the spectacle of the underground sky were a Maori chief, Tane Tinorau, and a British surveyor, Fred Mace, in 1887. The Maoris had already known of the existence of the grottoes for some time (the name in the local language is a combination of the two words meaning "water," *Wai*, and "hole," *Tomo*), but until then they

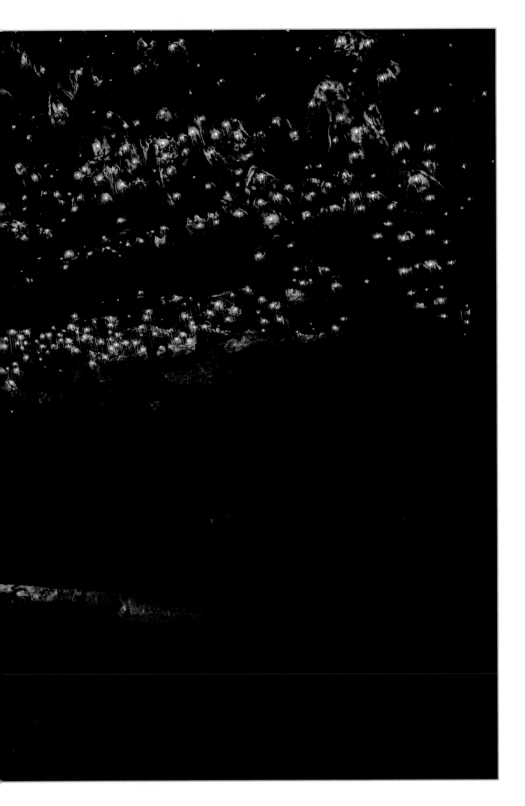

ADVICE FOR TRAVELERS

WHEN TO GO The grottoes are open all year, except for Christmas Day. Given the limited number of daily tours, the only way to visit them is by guided tour booked in advance.

HOW TO GET THERE The site of the grottoes is 125 miles from Auckland and 46 from Hamilton. They can easily be reached on main roads.

WHAT YOU NEED Comfortable anti-slip shoes, a warm jacket. Cameras are not permitted.

DIFFICULTIES These vary depending on the route and activities chosen: there is something for every interest and level of difficulty. Some routes are suitable for everyone, including families and children, while others are more adventurous and demanding.

WEB SITES
www.waitomo.com
www.newzealand.com/int/
waitomo-caves
www.hobbitontours.com

258-259 The romantic underground starry sky originates from the luciferin that reacts chemically with oxygen, thus generating cool light. The *Arachnocampa luminosa* was observed for the first time in 1871 in a gold mine in the Thames Region, not far from Auckland.

had never ventured into the underground caverns. Subsequent exploration led to the discovery of a higher access point to the grottoes, which is the one used at present. The simplest way to explore them is on foot or by boat, but adventure lovers surely cannot miss the rafting excursion or abseiling, for which good agility is

enough. Another touch of adventure: only a few minutes away by car are the Ruakuri grottoes: just as spectacular, they have a spiral entrance, built by nature with refined engineering perfection. There is also the smaller Aranui grotto with white stalactites, and the Marokopa falls announced by a distant roar.

There is a treat for the lovers of *The Lord of the Rings* trilogy: the grottoes are only an hour by car from Hobbiton, the Hobbit village constructed for the set of the film saga.

VOYAGE TO THE END OF THE OCEAN TO MEET THE PENGUINS

A FIERCE CLIMATE AND UNEXPECTED STORMS
GREET THE TRAVELER WHO DARES TO CROSS
THE LIMITS OF THE WORLD: THE FALKLANDS, SOUTH
GEORGIA AND SOUTHERN SHETLAND HOST COLONIES
OF BIRDS WHICH ARE ATTRACTED BY HUMANS.

Under a leaden sky, the "southernmost city in the world" has an the uncompromising aspect of wild lands. It is crowned by mountains which disappear into the titanium reflections of the Beagle Strait.

260 A huge column of royal penguins in St Andrews Bay, in South Georgia. Penguins are aquatic birds but incapable of flying; the fins they use for swimming were originally wings.

260-261 In search of food, shortly before diving into Antarctic waters. Emperor penguins feed on krill, shrimp and fish, even swimming 50 miles to catch them.

WHEN TO GO From November to March.

HOW TO GET THERE By plane from Buenos Aires with Aerolíneas Argentinas as far as Ushuaia, and then by ship.

WHAT YOU NEED The southern summer is characterized by mild temperatures, between 23 and 41 °F. During the storms, the temperature can suddenly drop, but it rarely goes below 5 °F. Winter mountain clothing is suggested. For going ashore, high thermal boots, which can be hired on board, are ideal.

DIFFICULTIES None in particular, and the crew does its best to facilitate moving from the ship to the dinghy, from the dinghy to land and vice versa. However, you should remember that these operations are performed on a very restless sea, in potentially lethal waters. It is better to undertake the voyage in good physical condition.

WEB SITES
www.antarctica.gov.au/
about-antarctica
www.nationalgeographic.org/
encyclopedia/antarctica
www.gov.gs/visitors/
how-to-visit-south-georgia

262 An elegant emperor penguin with his chick, which is still awkward and covered in soft, dense brown plumage.

263 Tourists watch a group of Papua penguins. This species is no taller than 3.5 inches.

Ushuaia was founded on October 12th, 1884 by an Argentine sailor sent here by Buenos Aires to plant the Argentinian flag in a Tierra del Fuego where the British were too present, and was a penal colony before it was a free port. Today it has about 57,000 inhabitants and is the most important starting point for cruises destined for the Antarctic, due to the comparative proximity of the southernmost point of Latin America (Cape Horn) to the northernmost point of the Antarctic Peninsula. Between them, there are only a thousand miles of storms answering to the name of Drake Passage.

To begin your search for penguin colonies, you board ships suitable for polar navigation, with specially reinforced hulls. They are mostly oceanographic research ships that are hired for the summer season for these particular cruises. The advantage of this style of traveling, which is certainly spartan compared to that of the few cruise ships that venture to these parts, is that these ships carry a limited number of passengers, with a very specialized crew. If you consider that only one hundred people at a time can land in Antarctica, you can easily understand the difference between a ship with 800 passengers and one with 80.

If you aim to get up close to the great penguin colonies, in particular the emperor penguin, you are advised to choose a cruise which includes South Georgia: to reach the nearest Emperor

penguin colony you have to cross the Antarctic Circle, a privilege reserved for few commercial ships. In Georgia, too, there are very few ships authorized to drop anchor, but there is a much better chance of finding yourself surrounded by thousands of penguins.

The typical cruise envisions the Falklands (Malvinas for the Argentinians), South Georgia, the Antarctic Peninsula with the Southern Shetlands, crossing the Drake Passage, rounding Cape Horn and, finally, re-entering the Beagle Channel to return to Ushuaia. It is about 3,500 nautical miles to travel in total contact with the wildest nature on the planet.

For twenty days you are exposed to a climate that can turn ferocious in a moment, and you need to protect yourself with suitable clothing.

Even when the sun shines and the temperature moves above zero, your backpack should contain thermal jackets, padded pants, caps and warm gloves, because storms come up suddenly.

There are precisely 339.4 nautical miles and 36 hours' sailing between Ushuaia and West Point Island, the first landing point in the Falklands. The voyage is accompanied by majestic albatrosses and numerous whales.

The Falklands appear as a slight distortion in a determinedly empty horizon. They are low, almost devoid of high vegetation, with many sheep.

There are 2,000 inhabitants, almost all in Stanley, the capital, and very many land mines. The latter are the result of the brief war between Argentina and the United Kingdom in 1982.

A pointless war, which was to leave a lasting trace in the future of these remote islands: to clear the islands of mines, it would be necessary to devastate the islands with bulldozers and destroy the nesting grounds of thousands of sea birds. For now, no one seems to want to do this.

On these islands you have your first encounter with the penguins, colonies of Rockhoppers, which feature an uncombed yellow and black tuft, like a rock star. They are curious animals and aren't bothered by human presence, so you can approach them easily.

It is 784 nautical miles and 60 hours'

With their polite bows, their monogamous love, the altruism that they demonstrate, they are sure to create that emotional involvement that ensures success.

Danilo Mainardi

Ethologist, ecologist, science popularizer

sailing from Stanley to the forbidding cliffs of South Georgia across the Sea of Scotland. At the beginning of the twentieth century, South Georgia became one of the main destinations for whalers, and this continued until the collapse of the industry in 1966. Today, South Georgia has no real towns, not even a runway, and is basically a nature paradise untouched by humans.

In Georgia there are three days of hard, unyielding nature. The best trips are those to Grytviken – where you can visit the imposing remains of the whaling station which, between 1904 and 1966, "processed" 175,000 whales, and to the tomb of Sir Ernest Shackleton.

The most intense moments of this coastal cruise around this natural fortress come at St. Andrews Bay and Salisbury Plain, where two huge colonies of royal penguins congregate. In both cases, landing depends on the proverbially ferocious weather conditions on this island. These are unforgettable moments: you find yourself in the presence of hundreds of thousands of penguins. You only need to move away

a little from the other visitors and lie down to be completely surrounded by hundreds of birds whose curiosity prompts them to touch even your pants and camera tripod with their beaks.

You look upward at them standing out against the sky, or you kneel down in the cold water while they return shoreward against the waves; finally, you watch them from the hills on the edge of the glacier: a river of living beings spreading onto the ocean shore in a sort of teeming delta.

And now comes the great leap toward Antarctica: after leaving the coasts of South Georgia, once more you follow Shackleton's route, via Elephant Island. Two more days on the open sea, 750 nautical miles, accompanied by distant horizons, thousands of birds, dozens of whales, and icebergs over 25 miles wide. There follow five days of pure Antarctic: endless spaces, whiteness and silence. The routes are marked by icebergs and mountains rising directly from the sea; landings are marked by close encounters with Chinstrap (*Pygoscelis antarcticus*) and Adelia

(*Pygoscelis adeliael*) penguin colonies. Excursions in dinghies lead to visions of glaciers, to gazing among the icebergs, to zigzagging along changeable corridors of floating ice, to close encounters with various types of seal.

Half Moon Island with its beauty worthy of a painting, Deception Island with its crater and bathing in thermal waters, Wilhelmina Bay, where the real Antarctic continent sets its foot for the first time, Cuverville and Petermann Islands, with their iceberg labyrinths: you soon lose track of the places and the emotions. Around latitude 65° 10' south, the bows turn north, through Drake Passage, in the direction of Cape Horn.

264 Four Chinstrap penguins follow a hiker's tracks. Despite their innocuous and gentle appearance, this small species is one of the most aggressive.

266-267 Papua penguins survey a small iceberg.

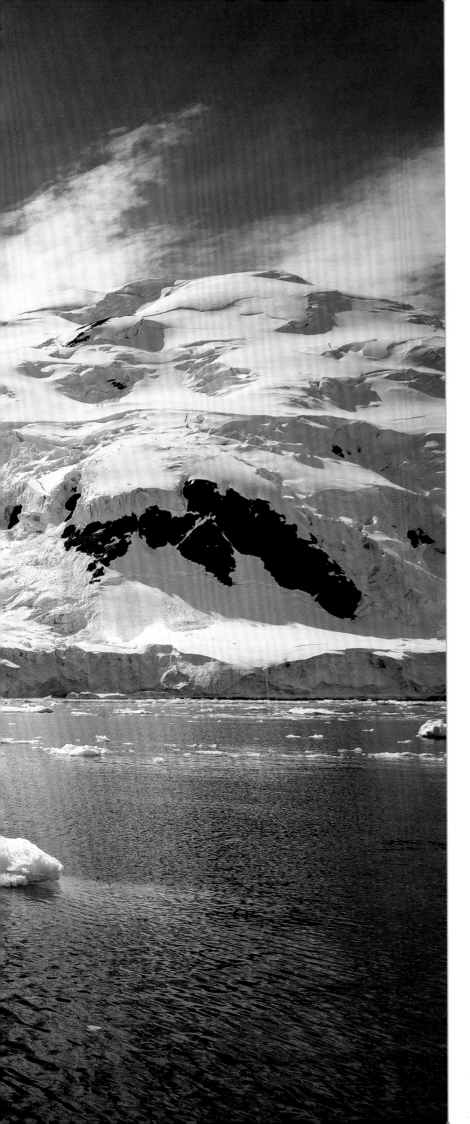

HOMAGE TO SHACKLETON

Sir Ernest Henry Shackleton was the famous British explorer who was trapped in his ship Endurance in January, 1915 in the Antarctic pack ice. He was attempting to reach the South Pole. The explorer and his companions managed to reach Elephant Island, in the South Shetlands. In 1916, Shackleton crossed 990 miles of stormy sea in a lifeboat with five companions. He left Elephant Island, miraculously reached the south coast of South Georgia, crossed over, through glaciers and rock walls, and finally arrived in Grytviken, after one of the most incredible exploits in human history.

He died some years later in this corner of the world. After visiting his tomb and paying tribute to his courage, you conclude with a curious ritual: you toast Shackleton in whisky or beer, and after one sip, you pour the rest of the glass on the tomb.

THE AUTHORS

Claudio Agostoni

Director of programming for Radio Popolare in Milan. He is the author of *Onde Road*, radio travel documentaries. He writes on travel and music for various publications in Italy and abroad. He is particularly passionate about the cultures and sounds of Africa.

Elvio Annese

Professor at the Accademia di Belle Arti di Brera (Milan), where he teaches montage, he is also the author of documentaries dedicated to musical, social, and geographical themes. In 2004 he was the screenwriter of the documentary *K2, une histoire italienne* (National Geographic prize at the Festival d'Autrans). He is the author of guides on Madagascar and Cape Verde for the ClupGuide.

Alessandra Bartali

A freelance journalist, she began travel writing in 2004, publishing two (non) tourist guides for the series ClupGuide on the two places that have been her home: Berlin and Tuscany. She travels and writes for various publishers and local and national magazines. She also writes on current themes and creates radio audio-reportages.

Alberto Bellani

A geologist with a long experience in the world of scientific research, he works with software, digital cartography, and geography, particularly with regard to environment and landscape, its forms and evolution.

Elena Brunello

She graduated in American Literature from the University of Edinburgh. Since 2012, she has collaborated with various Italian and international publications as a travel reporter. At present, she works as an author of documentaries. Her work has been selected for various documentary festivals in Belfast, Leeds, and Orvieto.

Beppe Ceccato

A journalist who has worked in magazines on travel, tourism, food and wine (*Dove, Weekend Viaggi, Viaggiesapori*), lifestyle (*VS*), and music (*Rolling Stone*). He has published tourist guides on Brazil for ClupGuide, and for Newton Compton, with A. Forlani, *101 viaggi straordinari da fare almeno una volta nella vita*. He takes his camera everywhere.

Alessandro Gandolfi

A reporter for *La Repubblica* until 2001, he is a photographer and journalist, and founding partner of the agency Parallelozero. His photos have appeared in international publications, from *Le Monde* to *Geo* to *Sunday Times Magazine*, and in personal and group exhibits. He is the Italian photographer with the highest number of reportages for *National Geographic Italia*. He has won the National Geographic's Best Edit Award four times.

Valerio Griffa

A journalist and photographer, he has collaborated with the main daily and periodical Italian publications. He has edited three online magazines, among which ViaMichelin, and collaborated with Radio Rai. He has published 15 books and participated in three photographic exhibits.

Elena Luraghi

A resident of Milan, her passion for architecture led her to earn a degree at the Politecnico di Milano. She was driven by curiosity to become a journalist. She writes travel books and lifestyle articles, and has won various prizes for the best "travel article" of the year.

Marco Moretti

Full-time traveler, he is a journalist specializing in travel reportages and environmental themes. He collaborates with *La Stampa* and manages the site ecoreport.org on the relationship between tourism and the environment. He has published 15 works (guides and geographical books). He has visited 130 countries and has won three international reportage prizes.

Paolo Paci

Chief editor and editor-in-chief of various monthlies, among which *Weekend Viaggi, Viaggiesapori*, and *La Cucina Italiana*. He divides his time between the Alps, Liguria, and Milan, where he lives with his wife, children, their cat, a turtle, and too many plants. He has dedicated a dozen volumes to nature and Alpine cultures: photographic books, monographs, and travelogues.

Violetta Polese

A journalist and translator, she has lived in Viet Nam, China, the Sudan and other countries, where she has explored the geography and culture. She has written tourist books and guides on the Netherlands and the Sudan, among others.

Serena Puosi

A Tuscan freelance copywriter with a passion for traveling, books and photography. More than ten years ago, she opened the blog *Mercoledì tutta la settimana*, where she relates her journeys around the world, first with her companion and then with her children.

Marco Santini

He has always been a traveler. He is a journalist, video-maker and photographer who specializes in travel reportages. He travels by motorbike, boat, and on foot, collaborating with the most important travel magazines in Italy and abroad. He has taught photography in the American School circuit and has staged various photographic exhibits.

Francesca Spanò

A journalist, television writer, and travel writer. She has worked for Sky, where she focused on travel documentaries. She is the blog manager of various tourism blogs. She collaborates with numerous Italian and international publications.

THE EDITOR

Gianni Morelli

He is the author of essays, guides, textbooks, novels, stories, and movie storylines. Regarding the theme of nature, he has worked in research institutes and written about journeys, geography, and history. For twenty years he was the editor of the series ClupGuide, for which he wrote many guides: on Mexico, Cuba, Guatemala, Costa Rica, Nicaragua, Peru, and Bolivia. He has written geography courses for Signorelli, Elemond, and Giunti TPV, and geographic and thematic atlases for DeAgostini and RCS. He has edited various publications for White Star; most recently: *Great Discoveries and Inventions That Have Changed the World* (2018). He edited *United States* for the National Geographic Traveler Guides. He is the director of the publishing firm Iceigeo in Milan.

ACKNOWLEDGMENTS

We have used the word "unique" more than once, but in the end it proved to be inevitable. We mean that after reviewing all the work together, we do not believe we have exaggerated with the superlatives, the "fantastics," the "extraordinaries," the "incredibles," and so on, as we feared we might. We "used" the texts of our colleagues who were "in the field": they wrote and we, disrespectfully, sometimes recast the pieces to bring them still closer to the concept of this volume. We can only thank them for this; we hope that they, too, are satisfied with the recasting, and that at the end of this volume they are as proud as we are, from the directors of the publisher, to the editing staff, to the graphic artists, and last (but not least) to the proofreaders.

Actually, the first to thank are probably those who, at their desk in the publishing house, conceived and approved the project. From then on, it was only a long struggle to propose, modify, re-propose, re-modify, persevere, until the final decision on what, who, how, how many was made. A war that exhausted us; but it was worth it. The pieces have no bylines, because we consider this a great team product. The more qualified and those who worked most, including the editor, have all been part of a collective creation. But each of them will know that he/she is in one or more of the pages that you are enjoying.

PHOTO CREDITS

Editorial project VALERIA MANFERTO DE FABIANIS and LAURA ACCOMAZZO

Graphic design MARIA CUCCHI

WS White Star Publishers® is a registered trademark
property of White Star s.r.l.

© 2019 White Star s.r.l.
Piazzale Luigi Cadorna, 6
20123 Milan, Italy
www.whitestar.it

Translation and Editing: ICEIGEO, Milan
(Translation: Jonathan West; Editing: James Schwarten;
Editorial staff: Chiara Schiavano, Lorenzo Sagripanti, Margherita Giacosa, Giulia Gatti)

ISBN 978-88-544-1346-7
1 2 3 4 5 6   23 22 21 20 19

Printed in China